How To Self-Publish Your Book For Free on CreateSpace & Amazon Kindle

Make Your Dream Come True!

Make Money Creating & Publishing eBooks on Amazon

Thomas Jerome Baker

Revised, ReEdited, RePublished June, 2015

ISBN: 1490326545
ISBN-13: 978-1490326542

DEDICATION

This book is dedicated to, and written for, all the people, worldwide, who want not only to create and self-publish eBooks for free, but also to make money. You can make your dream come true with Createspace & Amazon Kindle by using the knowledge in this book. Beginners and experts alike will find something of use and of value in this book to help you achieve your goals.

Unlike most "How To" books, this book is written as an experience, a true story to be shared. You come to this book not just for the steps, the "How To," but also to know my story, what it was like to self-publish without having the knowledge in this book. That's important, because it helps you to avoid mistakes.

Creating and publishing an eBook is a journey. Somehow, you never really "get there," reach the final destination (complete mastery), because we constantly discover something new that we can do better, do faster, do more effectively the next time.

I am still learning, but this book contains the story of how I gained the knowledge I wish I had known 100 books ago, when I self-published my first book. With this book in your hands, I know your creative process will be as good as mine is, today, and help you to make your dream come true to make money by creating and publishing eBooks on Amazon and CreateSpace.

Just as important, you will create not only your book(s), but also your own self-publishing story. You too will want to share your story and your knowledge to help others self-publish their book. So enjoy your journey to self-publishing your book for free and making money. As they say in French, "Bon Voyage!"

CONTENTS

ACKNOWLEDGMENTS

My wife, Gabriela, and my son, Thomas Jerome Baker, Jr. are the source of my inspiration to share my understanding of creating & publishing using Createspace & Kindle free author platform. I have published over 100 times, learning something new each time.

I can now share what works for me, because of the love and support I have from my family. Dear Reader, I know you will add your own experiences, your own true story, knowledge, skills and abilities to what I share with you in this book. In this way, you make it personal, you own your creative process, just as I have done.

Creating and publishing eBooks is personal, each book is literally a part of you. It is therefore your enthusiasm, your energy, your joy of creating and publishing that will determine your ultimate level of success. And that is well as it should be, that nothing and nobody can take your dreams away from you.

Again, Gaby and TJ, could there be any doubt that I would write in any other way, than personal, first person, when it is you who inspire me? Thank you for helping me to make my dreams come true. I love you both more than words can ever express...

CHAPTER 1
HOW TO SELF-PUBLISH YOUR BOOKS

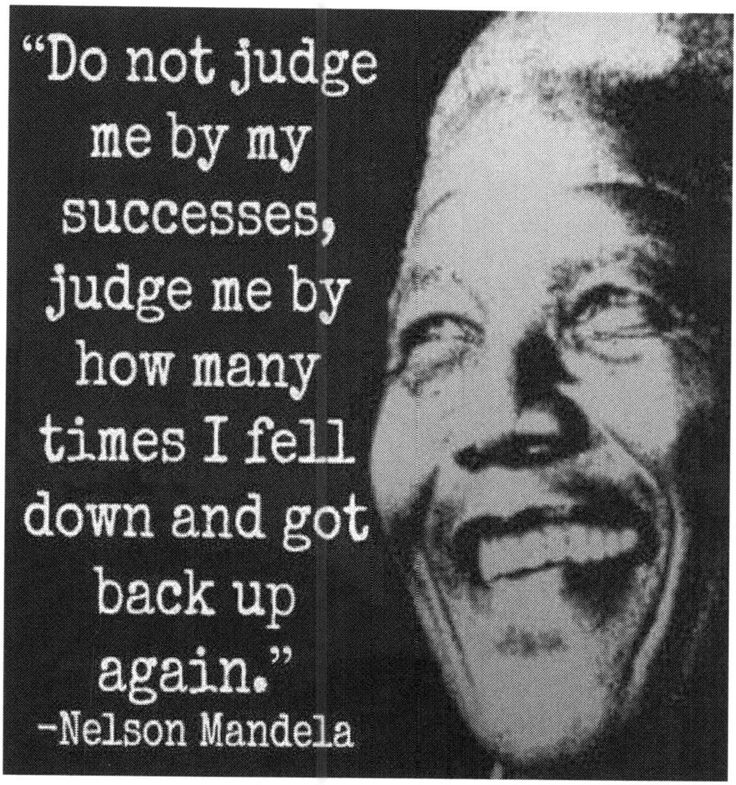

"Autodidactic" is defined, quite simply, as "teaching yourself". [From Greek autodidaktos, self-taught : auto-, auto- + didaktos, taught; see didactic.] (The Free online Dictionary). It's a concept that doesn't get much attention nowadays. It's almost as if it's not valid, to be your own teacher.

And then I do a quick Google search and the names of the people who are in the "Autodidact Club" literally take my breath away. Really, it's absolutely amazing. There are a wide diversity of accomplished, self-taught people. There are Presidents and Prime Ministers, musicians, architects, painters and poets, inventors, scientists, Nobel Prize winners, writers, actors and actresses, singers and dancers, and on and on.

If you press me for names then I answer thusly:

Nelson Mandela, Bill Gates, Steve Jobs, Walt Disney, Stanley Kubrick, Woody Allen, Walter Cronkite, Ted Turner, Steven Spielberg, Zachary Taylor, William Mckinley, Abraham Lincoln, George Washington, William Faulkner, William Blake, and…

Let me catch my breath. I'm just getting started. OK, let's continue:

Washington Irving, Walt Whitman, Vivian Thomas, Thomas Watson, Thomas Alva Edison, Samuel Clemens, Joseph Conrad, Joseph Campbell, Judy Crichton, Karl Rove, Laura Ingalls Wilder, Leo Tolstoy, Louisa May Alcott, Malcolm X, Martin Van Buren, Maya Angelou, Michael Faraday, Milton Hershey, Nikola Tesla, Soichiro Honda, Michael Dell, and…

I gotta take a break for some more air. This list is about halfway through, and I want to apologise in advance to all those people, whose names are not on this list, but most definitely belong here. Ready? Let's mention some more people:

The Wright brothers (Orville and Wilbur), Patrick Henry, Peter Jennings, Peter Ustinov, Quentin Tarantino, Ralph Lauren, Ray Bradbury, Benjamin Franklin, Ray Kroc, Richard Leakey, Robert Browning, Robert Frost, Ernest Hemingway, Estee Lauder, Florence Nightingale, F. Scott Fitzgerald, Frank Lloyd Wright, Gore Vidal, Grover Cleveland, David Ben Gurion, Harry Truman, Henry Ford, Herman Melville, James Monroe, James Cameron, Jane Austen, John D. Rockefeller, and …

Wow… Look at all these autodidactic people. Has education somehow missed the obvious? That maybe teaching isn't the only show in town? Has this kind of learning – the one in which the individuals teach themselves – not been as thoroughly understood – as it evidently deserves to be – understood?

On that thought, shall we? Let's add one last batch of names to our list of autodidactics, self-teachers. As we do, however, remember, bear in mind that these are the special ones, the celebrated ones. Again, how many more must there be, yet virtually unknown to you and I?

John Major, Robert Burns, Agatha Christie, Albert Einstein, Alex Haley, Alexander Graham Bell, Alexander Pope, Andrew Carnegie, Andrew Johnson, Ansell Adams, Beatrix Potter, Benjamin Banneker, Carl Sandberg, Charles Dickens, Chuck Yeager, Colonel Sanders, Doris Lessing, Edgar Allen Poe, Edith Wharton, Elizabeth Barrett Browning, William Shakespeare, Bob Dylan, Emma Goldman, Eric Hoffer, Abigail Adams, and Eleanor Roosevelt.

Teaching yourself… maybe there is something to that concept. Look, let me add two more people to the list. One, that's you, my friend. If you are reading this, then let's face it, we both know you are convinced that there is something of value that you will learn here, by reading this book, namely, "How to Teach Yourself to Publish Your Own Books For Free."

Yet let's be honest: I'm not teaching you. You, are teaching, yourself. You are teacher and learner. That's autodidacticism, self-motivation, self-interest which leads to new insights, new knowledge. I'm sure you will take away something from reading this book. Just like the mythical search for the Holy Grail, you will find something, gain some new knowledge. Inevitably, without a doubt, this knowledge that was hidden to me, that was opaque to me, will become totally transparent for you. The power to publish a book, is, was, and always has been, inside of you.

And what about that second person? Well, we both know I'm talking about myself. The very act of writing this book is an act of autodidacticism. I'm learning more about myself, learning more about what I know, and even more about what I don't know.

That fact actually explains each and every book I write now, I wrote in the past, I have ever written, and that I will ever write in the future, given the opportunity. The same is true for you.

We are learning more about what we know, by sharing it with the public, and thereby uncovering the areas that we either need or want to learn more about. Therefore, being autodidactic is a good thing, for me, and for you, if we look at it in this way. It makes us better, in a multitude of ways. Foremost is the creative process that we experience as we do this, as we write our book, together.

Yes, writing is an expression of creativity. We create a relationship between writer and reader. Hence, writing is dialogic, an interrelated dialogue between writer and reader, in which the writer and reader converse, separated in time and space.

Now, here's the big question: Has autodidacticism been exploited, by the formal education system, as a viable way to acquire knowledge, skills and abilities? Probably not, if your education is like the education I received. I never had a teacher walk into a classroom and say to me, "Thomas, today I want you to teach yourself how to write and self-publish a book." Yet that is exactly what we are doing. We are teaching ourselves...

So, let me rephrase the question: How do you teach someone, to teach himself / herself? In the end, isn't this kind of independent learning what the world has depended on for ages and ages, to move forward? Yes, it is. That's why you have acquired this book, because you believe it will help you to write and self-publish your own books, just like it helped me, just like it motivated me, to share with you. Trust me, you will write your own book, and self-publish it. That's the purpose of this book, to guide you to the knowledge that is necessary for you to take control of your destiny and make your self-publishing dreams come true. Now is the time. We begin now.

Here's a final thought: If all we ever did, was teach people what we already knew, and everyone was content with learning, what was already known, then we would still be living in caves, wouldn't we? Finally, I leave you with an autodidact, namely, Filippo Brunelleschi. Brunelleschi? Who is he? He's the man who had to teach himself how to build the largest domed cathedral in the world, over six hundred years ago, when such knowledge had been lost or destroyed, or worse, forgotten. He had to teach himself. Nobody knew how to do what he had to do. Nobody.

Obviously, his methods of teaching himself are interesting for you and I. In essence, we seek knowledge, classical knowledge about self-teaching, about being an autodidact. That brings us to Florence, Italy, to Giovanni Medici, to Cosimo Medici and the Medici family (Godfathers of the Renaissance), http://bit.ly/13tRoBV, and on to the architect Filippo Brunelleschi.

Through Brunelleschi, we seek to understand and employ the very same methods he used during the Renaissance, the Rebirth. We will use this knowledge to self-publish our books, today, in the 21st century. Thus, we learn how to be both teacher and learner.

Now, we will be looking at Florence's Basilica di Santa Maria del Fiore (Florence Cathedral) and its amazing dome built nearly six hundred (600) years ago by Filippo Brunelleschi. http://bit.ly/1aNMmm8 Finally, we see an animation of Santa Maria del Fiore (Florence Cathedral). The animation was created by Paul Groh http://bit.ly/13beZs1.

CHAPTER 2
A LESSON FROM THE PAST: FILIPPO BRUNELLESCHI, THE DOME OF FLORENCE & THE MEDICI FAMILY DYNASTY

In the PBS video, "Birth of a Dynasty", we saw that nothing could please the enemies of the Medici family more than the architect Filippo Brunelleschi failing to build the dome. Cosimo Medici is thrown in jail, sentenced to death, and later self-exiled after paying a bribe to save his life.

Filippo Brunellesch is thrown in jail too. Work on the dome stops completely. In fact, the dome seems to have become connected to the Medici family, a symbolic representation of failure. A return to the Dark Ages seems almost certain. As a consequence, for the dome, it will surely never be completed. How could it be, with Brunelleschi in prison, and the Medici family in exile?

Statue of Filippo Brunelleschi

That's the way the world is. Here in Chile, we say that, "when one person climbs above the others, the others pull you down." If we appreciate this way of looking at human nature, we learn to exercise wisdom, and caution, just as Cosimo Medici did.

When the time was right, he returned to Florence. Cosimo had been counseled by his father, the humble Giovanni, to wait to be called back to the city. "Do not be impatient, a time will come when the people demand that you return, not as a conqueror or a despotic ruler, but as a saviour", he reportedly said to Cosimo. Indeed, this is how the story of Cosimo's return played out.

For now, let us decipher the lessons I have presented. We see an introduction of sorts. We meet the Medici family, and their willingness to take calculated risks in order to achieve their ambitions. That notion, that great results are possible, if we are willing to take the necessary risks, is one that will sustain you as you begin to go down the path to writing and self-publishing. You are also ambitious, so the lesson is a personal one for both of us.

We move on, as Giovanni Medici takes the path of humility, in word and deed. His actions call little attention to himself. He goes so far as to ride on a donkey! Imagine that, a rich man riding a donkey!

For us, we learn that we must take the opportunity to be true to ourselves. Writing and publishing a book, is ultimately a value proposition. Just as Giovanni created value for the people and institutions that he backed with the financial support of the Medici family bank, your book must strive to create value, or it will not make money. This ancient story teaches us to create value.

We see Cosimo Medici wisely following in the footsteps of his father. He remembers the advice to be patient, and though exiled, does not return to his beloved Florence until he has been called back. Cosimo furthers the interests of his family through the patronage of the greatest artists of his time, wisely separating the personal lives of the artists from the interests which he was pursuing. This resulted in him treating artists as human beings, with loyalty and respect. The results achieved were outstanding.

What we learn is that you, the writer and artist, the creator and publisher of your own book, do not exist in a vacuum, isolated from other people. These other people, brothers, sisters, parents, boyfriends and girlfriends, wives and husbands, children and grandchildren, play a role in your ultimate success as a writer. Include them, in one way or another. Show your gratitude, for they enabled your success. It doesn't come based on individualism.

Finally, we see Brunelleschi raise the dome. He has brought a major miracle to pass. Nowadays, no one would marvel at his accomplishment. Yet I remind you that this architectural miracle happened 600 years ago, and it was amazing. The dome weighed 37 tons. It consisted of 4 million bricks, in a construction that was revolutionary, unequaled and nonexistent, until Brunelleschi built the dome. It was said that the shadow of the dome was over the entire Tuscany, Italy. Even today, few people would disagree.

Let us now name ten principles we want to consider:

1. Publishing your book will make some people jealous, so expect to be treated differently, by some people.

2. Show your gratitude to those who help you.
3. Be humble, and you will have fewer enemies.
4. Be innovative.
5. Create value with your books.
6. Study books from the past.
7. Trust your instincts.
8. Be persistent.
9. Experiment.
10. Make everything as simple as possible (but not simpler).

#1. Jealousy

We live in a world in which technology has given common people like you and I the ability to write and publish books. Everyone has somewhere within them the secret dream of writing a book, publishing it, and making money. Deep within us, consciously and unconsciously, exists the human necessity to live a life that matters, to be significant, to be remembered as a success.

One way to assure yourself that you will be remembered is to write a book. Long after you are gone from this life, with your bones turned to dust, you have the possibility to communicate your knowledge, your dreams, your thoughts, your story, to a generation born to the future. For some, that is as close to immortality as we can come, without actually being physically able to accomplish it.

For instance, let me mention the names of Plato, Socrates, and Aristotle. They seem like people we know, because we have read about them. They exist in books. They entered our way of thinking, our way of knowing, through their writing, and through what was written about them. We think of Platonic Love, the Socratic Method, the Aristotelian Approach (deduction).

We know of these three people through books. They have managed to "live" long past their "expiration dates". Through books, they have achieved immortality in our collective memory. That's the power of writing. As a writer, as an author, it is within your grasp. Is it of little wonder that some people might react to your status as a writer, with jealousy, to some extent? It is only human nature.

Expect it, and it won't be difficult to deal with.

#2. Gratitude

I owe my deepest and most profound expression of gratitude to two people. They have been fundamental enablers in every book that I have ever written. These two people are my wife, Gabriela, and my son, Thomas Jerome Baker, Jr. Firstly, Gaby, my wife, has unselfishly, time and time again, given me the time necessary to write as much and as often as I have. Writing a book, and then self-publishing, are time-intensive endeavours. Hours go by almost without notice as you are engrossed in carefully completing some task associated with self-publishing your written work.

These hours come on evenings, and late at night, and on weekends and holidays. It is a rare author, a self-published author anyway, who is completely dedicated to writing. Writing is a hobby, a past time, something you do after your day job is done. The day job pays the rent, buys the food, and covers the living expenses of most writers.

The available hours that remain should be dedicated to the maintenance of family and social obligations. Chief among these is the family itself, and especially spouses and children. These are the people who your free time rightfully belongs to. In my case, my wife has sacrificed many an hour, given up evening after evening, night after night, weekend after weekend, holiday after holiday, as I worked on what I promised to be, "my last book".

She smiled that sweet smile of hers, gave me a kiss, and let me write, self-publish, and promote my books. She brought me coffee, made sure the room I was in was warm if the weather was cold, cool if the weather was hot, brightly lit if it was late at night, or turned off the brightly burning light if the light of day was streaming in through the window. She did all those things that I did not notice, engrossed as I was, deeply, in some task. Again, without my Gaby, there would be no books.

My son, TJ, is another matter altogether. Like all fathers, I am proud to have a son. I selfishly named him Thomas Jerome Baker, Jr. when he was born. After all, the name had served me well. I was proud to be who I was, and I was sure, he would no doubt also be proud to be my son. Yet with the wisdom of hindsight, and advancing age, I now question if I would act in the same manner, if I were to have, magically, a second opportunity to name him.

I say this because, where I have difficulty singing the simplest of songs with some kind of harmony, every thing about him is musical. He sings as well as any singer I have ever heard sing, and I say that without fatherly bias. In essence, he has forged his own identity within the confines of having a name that suggests he would be the kind of person I am, serious, responsible, practical.

My students would have difficulty imagining me as a singer. I read, I write. I encourage, I promote, I believe in others abilities to achieve their dreams. I'm a rock to lean on for support when you need it. I'm a jumping off place after your wings are strong and will support you in flight. I teach, and I learn, yes, but I don't sing.

From this perspective, my son inspires me. Through his eyes, I see another way of being, in the here and now. Sometimes, it is more than acceptable to have no thought of what tomorrow holds in store for me. It is enough to be present, now, in this moment, and own it, completely.

You can see then that these two people, my Gaby, and my son, both perform two very important functions for me. Gaby's role enables me to be future oriented, considering present sacrifices in the hopes of achieving future accomplishments. TJ, my son, enables me to understand and appreciate the value of the present moment, and then make the effort to bring the two conflicting time elements, present and future, in harmony with the past.

Let me close by making the point that whatever you do, as a writer, it is never you, and you alone, who is responsible. Every second, of every minute, of every hour, of every day, impacts on the quality of life of another person. What we are called upon to do, as writers, taking on the tremendously time-consuming task of writing and self-publishing and promoting our books, is to acknowledge, with gratitude, the contributions of others. It's the least we can do, and believe me, it matters.

#3. Humility

Enemies are a fact of life. The effort to pacify your enemies is noble, and a worthy pursuit. Having said that, you will still have enemies as a result of your writing. Some people will not look kindly upon the fact that you have distinguished yourself as an author. These people could be your competitors, other people who somehow see you as their competition. It might be people close to you who used to see you as an equal, and now recognize that you have achieved something that they haven't.

We could go on and on, but the fact of the matter is that it is human nature to feel jealousy, and envy, for any number of reasons. How you deal with this is the way you show your true nature. Be kind to the same people you used to be kind to. Treat people, in word and in deed, by your acts and your omissions, exactly as you would like to have people treat you, and you will be least affected by jealousy or envy.

We know I'm talking about the biblical concepts of loving your enemies, and being able to be good to people who may not be treating you good. When we look into the Bible, and read it, *the first is from **Matthew 7:9-12**, and the second is in **Luke 6:27-31**.* When someone writes a bad review about your book, for example, instead of feeling bad, read these two Bible verses. They will help you to get past feeling mistreated. Love your enemies.

Sincerely, this works for me. If you are lucky, people who find fault with your book, for any reason, will write directly to you, contacting you through your email or other social media, and explain what they didn't like. This gives you an opportunity to go back to your original work, and in one way or another, address the issue. That is why it is useful to be open to criticism, make it possible for your readers to contact you, and then for you to take advantage of technology to improve your book, in some way.

Technology makes it possible for you to add comments, remove anything from your work that you judge to be unfounded or inappropriate in any way. In the old days, books could not be changed as rapidly, and as easily, as they can be today. Therefore, given this possibility, any reader of your book who objects to something you have written can address the issue directly with you, rather than by doing your efforts harm by writing negative reviews. As long as the issue is open, transparently, to direct dialogue between writer and reader, it is a much better value proposition than taking the avenue of advising other potential readers that your book is not worth the time or money to acquire.

However, as a writer, you must accept the inevitable (almost unavoidable) situation in which someone does not consider that writing a negative review exponentially decreases the probability that someone else might want to read your work. Remember, these are people who don't know you personally, so don't take it personal. Love your enemies.

On the other hand, when the people who react negatively to you or your book, then you have to exercise wisdom in dealing with the issue. My grandmother once told me there are two moments on life when you get to know people for who they really are: 1. When you are unsuccessful and in need of help, and 2. When you are successful.

In the first instance, you find your true friends remaining loyal to you, while other supposed friends desert you, and leave you, abandoned to your fate. In the second instance, you find yourself growing in popularity with people who never gave you the time of day before. What you have to do, in both cases, is remain true to yourself, and it will carry you through the experience.

You will be emotionaly and sentimentally intact, safe and sound, much better off than before, as a person. At least, now you know who you can depend on. Now you know who is worthy of your time, and who, sadly, isn't what you previously thought they were.

#4. Be innovative

In writing, everything has already been said. Everything has already been tried. Everything has already been done. There's nothing new under the sun. So, rather than recreate the wheel, do something ordinary in an extraordinary way. In other words, innovate. Use the old knowledge to create the new knowledge.

This book, for instance, is an innovation. We are learning important lessons through stories, not just lists of steps: Step 1, Step 2, Step 3, etc. It's because all of humanity is "hardwired" to interpret and understand stories in our collective memory.

For example: Tell your story in a voice that hasn't been heard before. Your story is your experience, your worldview, and it is uniquely shaped by your individuality. Your personality is unique, let it come shining through.

When Shakespeare came along, for instance, there was nothing new under the sun. It had already been said before, already been done before. Yet he managed to reshape English literature, not by being inventive, or creative, but by using the common words of the day in an uncommon way, by putting words and phrases together in such a way that they would be remembered easily, hundreds of years after his death. Where no words existed for what he wanted to say, then he invented new words!

No matter what you do, I can assure you, the world will be the better off if you tell your story in your voice. Tell your story through your eyes, and help your readers to feel emotions that you have felt. Connect with the needs, wants, and desires of your readers. Therefore, your greatest innovation may be nothing more than having the courage to be yourself, which is tremendous value.

#5. Value

Before I ever self-published a book, I knew I could write. I made my work available as free eBooks online. Literally thousands of people, from all over the world, downloaded my materials, my short stories, and my scholarly essays. At first, it was exhilarating, to get daily confirmation that my writing was reaching a global audience who was very enthusiastic about my work.

At first, I thought that it was only because everything was free. Gradually, it began to dawn on me that even free resources and materials have to create something of value for the readers. Otherwise, despite being free, it remains without value, worthless.

I developed a simple test, which I share with you, to determine if something I had written was valuable or not. I simply asked myself: "Is what I have written valuable for me, in some other way than subjective, sentimental value?" The best way for me to answer that question was by ensuring that everything I wrote was experiential, tested in my reality, with a minimum of philosophy. The reality of the world in which we live is what most people recognize as being valid, useful, and therefore of some intrinsic or extrinsic value.

Being an experiential, reality-based writer, beyond the resonance of the readers, meant that at the very least, everything I wrote had reflective value for me, and a high probability to serve a similar purpose for anyone who might decide to read what I had written. This approach to writing is how I create value, by creating first value for me, and by extension, value for another human being, facing the same situation or experience that I had faced.

#6. Study books from the past

As you begin to write your book, it is helpful to study what other authors have said about your topic in the past. In so doing, you know whether or not you are in agreement, or disagreement, with past writers. You know if you are going over ground that has already been covered, or in some way or another you are walking on ground that is new, untouched, or not covered sufficiently.

Further, you know if what you are saying is controversial, or not. If this is the case, you can then address the issues which are divergent in your view, and provide an explanation, hopefully grounded in evidence, that supports your point of view. In my field, English Language Teaching, there is a tendency for opinions to swing back and forth, almost like a pendulum. It goes without saying that what one may be practicing could eventually fall out of favor of the majority opinion. However, if your results are qualitatively equal to or superior to the majority opinion, it would then guide your decisionmaking as to what methods, approaches or techniques you would choose to use.

Another interesting point is the historical one, the sense of connectedness between now and yesteryear. The more you study books written in the past, to include the social, cultural, technological, economic conditions of the time period in which the book was written, the more you are likely to be able to avoid the pitfalls of the past, on the one hand, and take advantage of ancient knowledge, on the other hand. If we go back to Filippo Brunelleschi and the building of the domed church in Florence, we must acknowledge that it was the ancient knowledge that made his architectural innovations possible. He did new things with old knowledge. Don't shun the past because we live in a new world.

#7. Trust your instincts

We live in a time and an age in which data is readily available, current and up to date in most instances, on any topic we wish to seriously consider. Data is often irrefutable. Science is built upon empirical methodology, numbers which reveal the workings of our universe to us. I am a great believer in numbers, even though I admittedly have no love of numbers (I once turned down an offer of a scholarship to study engineering, 30 years ago, because I had no love for math).

However, when it comes to explaining human behaviour, forget the numbers. Quality, in anything, is subjective to the human condition. Humans are unpredictable, and counter to all practical expectations, the rational thing to do is to subject any book you wish to write to one and only one test question: Do *you* like it?

When you write about things you like, the chances are high that there are a large number of people, around the world, who probably like what you like as much or more even, than you do. How many singers, sing the songs they like? How many painters and artists, paint and draw what they like? We could go on all day like this, but the point is clear, namely, a tremendously large number of people like the same things we like. So trust your instincts to please yourself, and in so doing, you will also be doing the same for a large number of people.

#8. Be persistent

Never give up. We are talking about your dream. Dare to dream your dream, to go for it, to be singleminded about the object of your desire. Do not pay any attention to your naysayers, your cynics and critics. Do not let the people who do not believe in you, do not support you, do not let these people cause you to let your dream of writing & publishing your moneymaking book slip away.

If you need inspiration, I invite you to watch the persistence of ants, busily working on a hot summer day. The entire colony of ants, each one dreaming of a cozy winter, is working. Bit by bit, crumb by crumb, they relentlessly go about preparing for the winter. They know that only by persistence will they be successful.

In the face of all difficulty, persist. When it rains, persist. When it snows, persist. When it's hot, when it's cold, persist. Never stop believing in yourself, even when all around you, everyone has given up hope on you. If your dream is to be a self-published author of a moneymaking book, you are the only one who can make it happen. Be persistent.

#9. Experiment

This may be the easiest, or the hardest thing to do. In self-publishing, you can try anything. Let me repeat that. Anything and everything you can think of, your formula for writing and publishing your book can be totally different from what you read in this book. Trust me, that is fine with me. This book seeks to enable you to self-publish your book, using the approach I have used, or any other approach that you can think of after coming into contact with the information in this book.

I would make one recommendation though. Experiment consciously, with an awareness of where you start from. Be methodical, changing one element at a time, and notice the results each change has on your overall success. The technology you have at your disposal allows you to change titles, covers, blurbs, author name, wording chapters, length, everything is within your power to experiment. Just as I share with you my formula for self-publishing, it is within your power to make any adjustment or modification that you feel is necessary.

#10. Simplicity

Einstein said to keep things as simple as possible, but not to go beyond that. When I was in the military, we called that the “KISS” rule: Keep It Simple, Stupid. Let’s not beat a dead horse. How many people can drive a car, but don’t have the slightest clue about how an engine works? Obviously, it isn’t necessary to know how an engine works. Get in the car, put the key in the ignition, and turn it. The car works, so who cares about the engine?

In writing, detailed explanations are rarely necessary. When it does become necessary, however, be precise, orderly, and organised. Then return to whatever is needed to move your story, or your text, along to something infinitely more interesting than how the engine of the car works. Your readers will appreciate it.

Conclusion

We looked at ten points to consider in this chapter. They are principles to consider, nothing more, and nothing less. If you have considered these points, prior to actually experiencing them, they will make your transition from unpublished author to self-published author a more enjoyable experience.

We go from here to the knowledge of how to self-publish your book. It will change your life forever, being an author, a person who has published a book. For some, it will surely bring riches, fortune and fame. You are in the minority, however. For many of you, it will bring neither fortune, nor fame, and no glory. For all who read this book, what it does do is open the door wide open to the fulfillment of your dream. That fact alone is worth the effort it will take to self-publish your books.

In the next chapter, we will begin by looking at that moment when you are notified that you have successfully published your book and begin to work our way back, from the end, to the beginning. This is a new way to look at self-publishing, starting from the end of the process, and moving to the beginning afterwards. I call this, "Starting With the End in Mind." It's nothing more than knowing where you want to go, so you will make the correct decisions about the path you will take to reach your final destination.

CHAPTER 3
CONGRATULATIONS! YOU HAVE SUCCESSFULLY PUBLISHED ON AMAZON KINDLE DIRECT PUBLISHING!

We begin this chapter with the pleasant news that a book that I have written has been successfully published on the Amazon KDP. Here's what the actual email message (that you will receive when you publish your book) looks like:

Hello from Amazon KDP!

The book "**Teaching & Learning English** in **Chile**: What Every Teacher Should Know" you recently submitted to KDP and enrolled in KDP Select has been published to the Kindle Store and is already available* for readers to purchase here.

KDP Select allows you to enjoy benefits, such as earning a share of a monthly fund when readers borrow your book from the Kindle Owners' Lending Library and a promotional opportunity to offer your book as free to readers for up to 5 days every 90 days to expand your reach.

For more details on KDP Select, check out this page.

You can check on the current month's KDP Select fund by visiting your Bookshelf.

Also, you can find your book's number of borrows in real time through your Month-to-Date Unit Sales report here.

Now that your KDP Select-enrolled book is live, you can manage its free promotion days in your Bookshelf by clicking the "Manage Promotions" link from the "Actions" menu or from the "Edit book details" page.

Your book's initial enrollment in KDP Select lasts for 90 days. For your convenience, your book's enrollment will be automatically renewed for another 90 days, unless you cancel automatic renewal by un-checking "Automatically renew this book's enrollment in KDP Select for another 90 days" box under "Enrollment Details" of your book before your book's current enrollment term expires.

Take a peek below at other great author resources to help you sell more books:

Create a Dedicated Author Page for Yourself
http://amzn.to/Qxmoec

If you are this book's author, increase your sales potential on Amazon by creating an Author Central account and share your most up-to-date information via a dedicated author page. Publishers, be sure to work with your authors to set up their Author Central accounts, as well. Click the links below to create author pages on different marketplaces.

Amazon.com Amazon.co.uk
Amazon.fr Amazon.de

Create a Print Book with **CreateSpace** (a member of the Amazon group of companies) https://www.createspace.com/

Create print editions of your book using CreateSpace's full array of services to help you self-publish and make your book available for sale to millions of potential customers on Amazon.com and other channels by visiting here.

Join Our KDP Community

We host KDP Forums, which are a great place to learn from others and share your experiences about independent publishing. Click here to check them out.

If you need to update the price of your book, click here, or its descriptive information, such as title, author, or description, click here.

For additional ideas on how to merchandise your book, be sure to check out this page.

Thanks again for choosing KDP to publish your work; we wish you the best of luck in promoting and selling it!

Regards,
Kindle Direct Publishing

Connect with KDP and other Authors and Publishers on Facebook
Follow us on Twitter

*Please note that the product description may take up to 24-48 hours to appear on the detail page, and links to the book's physical counterpart may take up to five days. If you are resubmitting your content file or updating your book details, the changes should display live within the next 24-48 hours.

(End of email)

**

Well, this is the message that says you have completed an important stage in your journey to achieve your dreams. That is what this message tells you. you have created your book. You have published your book on Kindle. Next, you can begin to make money on your book.

Your options are to do nothing, or follow the advice given by Amazon Kindle to market and sell your book. It is definitely a good idea to have an Amazon Author Page. Take advantage of the promotional opportunity that this Amazon platform provides you, as I have done. http://amzn.to/Qxmoec

If you have not already published a paperback book on CreateSpace, you should take advantage of the relationship they have with CreateSpace to increase the global reach, or distribution of your book. In essence, your book is now available for sale to about a billion people.

It's a good idea to use social media. You should have your own Facebook page and your own Twitter account. It follows quite naturally that it is a good idea to follow Amazon KDP on social media (Facebook and Twitter), to stay current and up to date.

For example, Goodreads was acquired by Amazon. This is news found on Author Central. I recreate it below, so you will know that valuable information is available in many locations:

Author Central News: **Amazon to acquire Goodreads**
March 28, 2013 1:22 PM

Hello –

We're happy to announce that Amazon has reached an agreement to acquire Goodreads, a leading site for readers and book recommendations that helps people find and share books they love.

Amazon http://www.amazon.com/ and Goodreads http://www.goodreads.com/ share a passion for reinventing reading, a love of books, and an appreciation for the authors who write them. We both work every day to help authors like you reach a wider audience and make a better living at your craft, and together with Goodreads we intend to build many new ways to delight authors and readers alike.

We're excited to help create an even more powerful offering for all of our authors, and we hope you are too. You can read more in the press release here and the blog post from Goodreads here.

Best,
The Author Central Team

***

What I want to do next is show how I use my blog to amplify this message and ensure that the word gets out to as many people as possible who I am connected to, and hopefully, to other people who my connections are connected to. Here, it is important that many authors are having excellent results without having a blog.

Their success obviously validates their statements that a blog is not a necessary marketing tool. I have my blog, however, because I write on a number of topics and share it with the people who are connected with me through various social media.

I use the free Wordpress platform, which is more than sufficient for my purposes. Nonetheless, when I decided to make a serious effort to "brand" myself, the route I chose was to upgrade my free blog to the one I am using now, http://profesorbaker.com . The host remains Wordpress, but the wordpress attachment is no longer a part of the site URL.

Again, this is not necessary if you simply are in the experimenting phase. If you are unable to attract readers to your blog / website, it would be unwise to upgrade. The expense would not be justified, even though it is less than $20 dollars per year. If you consistently draw more visitors to your blog, at least 100 per day, day in and day out, then I would advise you to go ahead and "brand" yourself, and your books, by upgrading your blog.

Below you see how I have made a blog post to share the good news with the readers of my blog. The information is promotional in nature. The heading, or title, comes from the heading of the email I have received from Amazon KDP. It is the kind of title that draws attention immediately to it. When we congratulate someone, for anything, it is a moment to be proud of, and therefore most people find themselves attracted to the headline to find out what the good news is all about:

**

Congratulations, you've successfully published on the Kindle!
Teaching & Learning English in Chile:

http://amzn.to/XYX2xP

This book is dedicated to all the people who are or have ever been students of a foreign language, in any classroom, around the entire world. The learning of a foreign language is a long, slow, labor-intensive process, requiring enthusiasm, motivation, dedication and perseverance, over many years.

Beware of anyone who would have you believe that English, or any language for that matter, can be learned in 3 weeks, 3 months, or even 3 years. They are not to be trusted, for the learning of a foreign language is never complete. It takes a lifetime of learning…

I believe there are 4 things every teacher of English should know:

1. The Mother Tongue
2. Educational Leadership
3. The National English Test
4. Connectivism

I therefore set out in this book to bring these four topics together, in sequential fashion. The "Mother Tongue" responds to research that says teaching English, in English, is how we get our best results. "Educational Leadership" fills a gap by raising our awareness of our individual leadership capacity, while the "National English Test" is how we are currently defining the quality of our teaching on a collective, national level. Finally, "Connectivism", as a theory of learning for a digital age, gives a view of what the future holds up as a promising way forward in ELT pedagogy. http://bit.ly/11sKkps

I am sure you will be enriched by the reading of this book. Forgive me if I am mistaken. Still, I entertain the sincere hope that you enjoy the journey of discovery that lies before you as you read this book…

To write and publish such a book as this one, there is an army of people who play a role. In self-publishing, however, there is an army of one.

I am that "army of one" in this instance. I felt a need to bring together four topics which are rarely spoken of in ELT in any consistent or exploratory manner, though by no means taboo topics: 1) The Mother Tongue, 2) Leadership, 3) The National English Test, and 4) Connectivism.

My hope, obviously, is that this book will make a contribution to fill the existing gap in reflection, dialogue, and ultimately, in our practice.

Self-publishing, as we can see by my example, is a valid way for teachers to ask questions, raise issues, explore profoundly, consistently, and durably, to inform the knowledge and practice of other teachers.

It is with this in mind that I encourage other like-minded teachers to self-publish, and I rejoice in your contribution to the development of our knowledge about what works best in English Language Teaching. http://bit.ly/11I88GH

**

In this chapter, we have taken the unusual step of beginning at the end of the process. When you are notified that you have successfully published your book on Amazon KDP, the team sends you an email message of congratulations. Your journey to self publish has ended successfully.

A new journey begins. Your book will now need to be promoted, and marketed, if you are to achieve a significant number of sales. Since making money is part of the dream, we must now seriously concern ourselves with getting the word out to as many people as possible. Yet the promotion of your book is another matter entirely to be considered, from a number of different perspectives. We looked at some of the basic steps to take to begin to promote your book, and they should not be ignored.

However, I want to remind you, the writer, that now is a very good time to pause. What is important now, at this time, is the celebration of your success. Writing a book, and then self-publishing it, is worthy of celebration. So go ahead, and broadcast the good news to your friends and family. You are a published author now, and make no mistake about it, the fact that you self-published your work does in no way, shape or form detract from your accomplishment.

Traditional publishers publish books they believe they will be able to sell. They have done market research, identified a niche they wish to compete in, engaged their entire team to ensure your writing meets the standards the reading public is accustomed to, and produced a product they believe they can sell, and sell well. The process of a traditional publisher, from beginning to end, usually takes between one and two years, from manuscript to publication.

As you look at this estimate of how much time goes by, it becomes quite clear why few people achieve their dreams of getting their work published traditionally. It's quite a long, exhausting process. A lot of resources, both material and financial, have to be invested. There is a possibility that your book, after being published, printed and shipped off to the physical stores where it will be placed on shelves to be displayed and sold, well, maybe it won't sell as many copies as anticipated.

Under such circumstances, risks with new authors are to be avoided. Unsold books means losses. Losses mean no royalty payments for the author, unwanted books to be resold at bargain basement prices, and in the worst cases, unemployed workers, and closed book stores.

Yes, book stores are closing, even the ones you thought were doing well. On February 5, 2013, the following headline could be read in the online version of the Atlantic, an influential newspaper: "**The Endangered Fate of Barnes and Noble**." The following statement caught my attention: "Barnes & Noble is the last bookstore chain standing," Wharton management professor Steve Kobrin, who is also the publisher of Wharton Digital Press, told the *Knowledge@Wharton* newsletter. "There's still a niche there, but it may go to small independent bookstores." http://bit.ly/1aSgrB8

More recently, June 12, 2015, an article in the New Yorker caught my attention. Titled, "When A Bookstore Closes, An Argument Ends," it made the case that when a bookstore closes, it is a loss to freedom.

(Quote) "I happened to find myself in Paris last week and went to look one last time at an almost seventy-year-old bookstore called La Hune, on the Place St.-Germain des Prés. I knew that it would be closing for good, though I was surprised to find that its *fermeture definitive* was to be this week, on Saturday, June 14th. I walked through La Hune one last time, sniffing the books and looking at the posters, and found myself far more distraught than I expected to be. I felt a deep sense of loss, more than mere regret, and ever since I have been trying to decide why I felt this way and whether the feeling was mine alone or might have resonance elsewhere." (end of quote)

The author goes on to state what caused this store to close, namely, the internet. Amazon did it. Author Adam Gopnik continues,

"Bookstores open and they close, following the path of bright young people as migratory birds follow the sun. In Paris, good bookstores have opened in, or migrated to, the popular *quartiers* of the 15th and 19th arrondissements, just as a few independent bookstores in this city have migrated to the sunnier climes of Brooklyn. Anyway, a bookstore is only a platform for the purchase of literature, and platforms move and change with every new age, gathering and then shedding the moss of our memories as they roll on." (end of quote)

We must insist on finding out why closing a bookstore is a loss to freedom. Gopnik explains thusly: (quote) "...why closing a bookstore is a loss to freedom, is that free-market societies...have built, alongside the responsive market with its unending appetite for change, smaller institutions where people can exchange ideas, share spaces, be in contact, feel at home, without any particular institutional endorsement from higher authorities. Restaurants, bookstores, cafés...are the sinews of civil society. The great German post-Marxist philosopher Jürgen Habermas...believed that those intermediate institutions were where the real work of eighteenth-century mind-making got done. Enlightenment happened more often in a café than a classroom. It still does." (end of quote)

Let's move now and take a look at England. The "Guardian" newspaper reported that more than 500 bookstores had closed since 2005 (source: Booksellers Association, 21 February, 2014).

(Quote) "Everyone should sit up and take notice of this," said Tim Godfray, chief executive of the association. "The book trade, the government and the general public need to realise that if we don't take action now, the future of our bookshops – and therefore the health of the publishing industry and reading itself – is at risk." (end of quote)

In March of this year the "Guardian" reported that little more than 100 independent bookstores remain in London. http://www.thelondonbookshopmap.org/ Is this the final chapter for London's independent bookstores? It depends on how you look at it.

(Quote) "It's not just the internet and rent hikes that's to blame. As Londoners in particular get more and more used to living in smaller spaces and to living in small rooms in shared houses well into mid-life, people just don't have the space for books any more and the Kindle solves that problem." (Peter Nexus, March, 2015)

Enough doom and gloom about bookstores closing. Don't we have enough evidence already to know that now is the time for authors like you and I to finally get our books published, free, and available for sale on Amazon (eBook) and CreateSpace (paperback)? We have the technology available, and it's not rocket science. If I can do it, you can too. We can do it. Yes. We. Can.

You and I have the opportunity, now, to go from isolation, being unknown, unwanted and unloved, out of the darkness of night, where we were seen as too risky for a traditional publisher to take a chance on, into the light of day, where we are creators and publishers, capable of making lots of money. Yes. We. Can.

Self-published authors now have opportunities to make money by creating, publishing and selling our books, the very same books we were previously content to give away, anything to have someone actually read our work. Those days are gone, and book stores are closing. Yes. Book stores are closing.

The horse and buggy of the past gives way to the automobile. History repeats itself. Now you see why I urge you to understand the story of the Medici family, of the Renaissance, and of Filippo Brunelleschi in particular.

As a self-published author, using the Print On Demand (POD) system, there is no risk, neither for the author, nor for the publishing company / vendor. All of those risk issues, the question of whether or not someone will buy your work, is now irrelevant. Physical resources, to include money, materials and people, are only used after a sale has been made.

Your book is printed on demand (POD). That means when someone wants your book, and uses their credit card to pay for the book, online, then the book is printed. There is no physical inventory, and the risk is zero, absolutely 0%, nothing. There will be no losses for your publisher, or for you, the author who is self-publishing all your books, for FREE.

Now, many authors decide to order a large number of discounted books, and then sell books themselves. They go to conferences, have seminars, workshops, even sell out of the trunk of their cars in some instances. As I said before, that is a consideration for another separate book, selling and promoting your book. I do not recommend this for the weak at heart, for people who have little financial resources.

What ***is*** important here is that you have been successful. You have self-published your book, and you deserve to celebrate with everyone who supported your efforts, in any way.

So, share the good news. Don't keep it to yourself. Call everyone whose telephone number you have. Email all of your personal contacts, including family, friends, and colleagues. Ask them to share the news with their families, friends, and colleagues.

Next, go to your social media. Get on Facebook, Twitter, LinkedIn, Pinterest, Tumblr, Instagram, Vine, YouTube, TeacherTube, Google+ and any other media you have at your disposal. Let this huge army of people know that you have published a book, and would be grateful if they bought a copy.

After you do that, your job is finished. You wrote your book. You published it. You promoted it. You are making money, good money. Well done my friend. Welcome to the ranks of self-published authors. You now belong to the Medici family of the 21st century.

You are an entrepreneur, just like Giovanni Medici, just like Cosimo Medici. With a little luck, a relative of yours just might become like Catarina Medici, Queen of France. Or the Pope, and I say that historically, as two Medici brothers became Pope of the Catholic Church, but that's another story for another book.

When you tell your family, friends, relatives and colleagues that you published your book, don't mumble. Speak clearly, and confidently. You have earned the right to be proud, yet humble, about your accomplishment. So, say with pride in your voice, "I am a self-published author."

Continue on: "You can find my book on Amazon Kindle, or if you want me to autograph a printed copy of my book for you, you can buy a paperback book from Createspace, my paperback publisher."

Inevitably, someone will remark that it's not the same thing as being published by a traditional publisher. Hold your ground, and say with humility, but informatively, "I know. I make 70% royalty on my book. Writers published by traditional publishers are lucky if they get 20%."

Then be quiet.

Next, maybe they might remark that it is a good thing to get 70%. A 70% royalty is only fair for all the time you invested in writing your book. After 2 years of working on your book, you should be paid well.

Please do your best to sound humble when you say, "I published my book in 2 days, not two years. The writing was easy, it was the preparation of the digital format that took me so long."

Final thought: Remember to be humble. Always. Be. Humble.

***

CHAPTER 4
HOW I PUBLISHED MY FIRST BOOK

To begin at the beginning, I must share the day I seriously began to investigate the possibility of self-publishing. The date was February 1, 2012. I had responded to a blogpost by Scott Thornbury, in which he announced Apple's plan to launch electronic publishing of school textbooks. An excerpt of what I wrote on my blog is below http://bit.ly/15qRigi :

I regularly read blogs of ELT professionals (every day) in order to stay up to date ("be the first to know") on what is happening in my field. Scott Thornbury in his excellent blog, An A-Z of ELT, is always a source of knowledge, inspiration and reflection for me.

His latest post, E is for eCoursebook, was no exception. I quote his opening sentence: "Apple's plan, announced last week, to launch electronic publishing of school textbooks set social networks a-twitter, triggering flurries of excitement and apprehension in equal measure." (end of quote) This post caused many people to share (as usual) their reflections."http://bit.ly/15qRigi

Further, the text of my response to Scott's blogpost, dated January 29, 2012 can be found here http://bit.ly/17L2Jnr in the response section immediately following the blogpost, about midway down the page. My response was one of 78 responses, showing that this was an extremely interesting topic for English Language Teachers.

In essence, since I did not own either an iPad or a Mac, I wasn't going to go out and buy one just so I could start self-publishing. Something inside of me rebelled at being forced to buy another set of hardware to do what I was already doing, namely, create content. I reasoned in my response that many people would feel the same way as I did.

Yet here is where I began to do some serious research into self publishing. I scoured the internet, reading everything I could find about self-publishing. The first piece of the self-publishing puzzle I would soon find. My objective was how to self-publish without buying a Mac or an iPad. Here is what I found, namely, Mr. Mark Coker, Founder of "Smashwords":

Smashwords' Mark Coker on E-Publishing http://bit.ly/17L5jtv Feb 20 2012

Twitter: https://twitter.com/#!/markcoker

Mark Coker: Founder of Smashwords, an ebook distributor. Also angel investor, gardener, hiker, battler of squirrels, dreamer, doer, co-author of, "Boob Tube" (A Soap Opera Novel) http://bit.ly/11jo1Dq .

Ebook publishing presents a tremendous opportunity for writers with an entrepreneurial spirit, those who are willing to not only write the book but market and distribute it. One of the many distribution options is Smashwords, which distributes over 100,000 ebooks on behalf of 37,000 indie authors, publishers, and literary agents. https://www.smashwords.com/

Ebyline chatted with Mark Coker, founder of Smashwords, about where the self-publishing world is headed. http://bit.ly/17L5jtv

What are the pros and cons of journalists self-publishing an ebook vs. signing with a traditional publisher?

MC: With self-publishing, journalists have the ability to out-publish, out-distribute and out-sell the large publishers.

The primary benefits of self-publishing are 1. immediacy, 2. control, 3. flexibility and 4. economics.

Immediacy:

At Smashwords, a journalist can upload their completed manuscript and ebook cover image and within 5 minutes it'll be made available for immediate worldwide discovery, sampling and sale from Smashwords.com. Within two weeks, we'll distribute that book to most of the big retailers, including the Apple iBookstore, Barnes & Noble, Sony, Kobo and others. With traditional publishing, most books appear. Most traditional publishers take 12-18 months to get a book out.

Control:

Self-pubbed authors retain all rights to their works, full editorial freedom and can price their content more competitively than traditionally published books.

Flexibility:

Self-pubbed ebook authors are not constrained by the typical word counts of print books. Journalists can write to the word count that makes the most sense for each piece. They can publish short form content of only 1,000 words, or longer form content of 250,000 or more words. The author has the freedom to update and iterate their content at any time. If they don't like their cover image, they click a link and upload a new cover. If they want to experiment with pricing, or a revised book description, they simply click a link. At Smashwords, we give the author full control over every aspect of their book from their Smashwords Dashboard, and the changes they make at Smashwords automatically propagate out to our retailers.

Economics:

A self-published book will earn the journalist between 60 and 80% of the list price as their per-unit royalty. Journalists have the ability to earn nearly same per unit selling a self-pubbed $5.99 ebook (earn $3.60 at 60% list) than they'd earn selling a $25 hardcover ($3.75 at 15% list). A traditionally published ebook priced at $12 would earn the author only about $2.10 (17.5% list, assuming a best case) from a traditional publisher.

The immediacy and flexibility of self-published ebooks allows writers to quickly respond to reader trends and interests, and also quickly monetize their writing.

How has the e-publishing landscape changed over the last few years? Has it become more mainstream?

MC: Four years ago when we started Smashwords, self-publishing was seen as the option of last resort. Self-published authors were considered the black sheep in the writing community. Today, self-publishing is becoming the option of first choice for many professional writers. It has definitely become mainstream. Our authors are scaling the bestseller lists at every major bookstore, and in the process they're inspiring the next generation of indie authors. A few weeks ago, one of our authors, Darcie Chan, was the #1 bestseller at the Apple iBookstore. Self-pubbed authors are also landing in the New York Times bestseller list for ebooks. The few who've made it there have become indie celebrities. In the next couple years, indie authors on the NYT list will become commonplace.

Any recommendations on setting prices for ebooks? We've seen prices over all the map.

MC: There's no general rule, other than perhaps to price lower than print. We publish over 100,000 books ranging from FREE to over $100.00. The average price of purchased books is $2.95 for us, and for any mathematicians out there, the median is about $2.90. Keep in mind the author retains 60-80% of that.

The best-selling, highest-earning authors at Smashwords are publishing multiple full-length books, and they use a range of pricing to simultaneously build platform and harvest sales. Lower prices are good for platform building. A price of **FREE** is an incredibly powerful platform building strategy.

If you publish multiple titles, at least one should be priced at free, and then you can use that to generate reader trust as well as demand for the other works that carry a price. Use the free and low cost titles to generate readership and reader trust (two essential elements of platform building), and then price others in your catalog higher to harvest income.

There are multiple other factors to consider beyond price, most of which I summarized in a guest post over at The Savvy Book Marketer titled, Pricing Strategies for Ebooks.

What are the biggest mistakes that self-published ebook authors make? Not polishing their manuscript, using an amateur-looking cover, something else?

MC: Those are excellent examples. I wrote a blog post at Smahwords titled, The Seven Secrets to Ebook Publishing Failure in which I documented the most common mistakes of self-published authors.

Where do you see epublishing headed over the next several years? Will we start to see more interactive or multimedia ebooks, cheaper e-readers, and so on?

Mark Coker predicts:

Market Growth: According the research from the Association of American Publishers, ebooks account for about 20% of the overall book market in the US today, up from about 8% a year ago and 3% a year before that.

Obviously, this exponential growth cannot continue forever. We'll see the growth rate slow, but I think we'll still see impressive growth over the next few years. There's a larger macro trend at play here: Reading is moving to screens. Screens are the new paper.

For 2012, ebook will probably approach 30% of dollar sales, and maybe 40-50% for 2013. From a unit consumption basis, ebooks will probably eclipse print by early next year since ebooks are priced less than print books. If you include downloads of ebooks priced at **FREE**, it's possible that consumption curve has already crossed over.

The market for ebooks outside the US is about 3-4 years behind us, so those markets are now just entering the most rapid phase of their exponential growth. With the next couple years, the market for English-language books outside the US will eclipse the US market. Already, we're seeing this trend at Smashwords. We distribute over 70,000 ebooks to Apple, who operates in 32 different countries. Nearly 50% of our sales are already outside the US. As Apple opens more international stores, and as these new markets proceed along their growth curve, international will open up in a big way.

Interactive:

I'd estimate that 90% of book sales are probably simple books, primarily straight reflowable narrative, and narrative plus images. They don't need interactivity, nor are readers clamoring for it.

Sales of interactive books have been disappointing for most publishers, and it's not a category we currently distribute. These books are more expensive to produce and they can't yet be distributed across all platforms. In the next couple years, we'll see better, cheaper tools for creating these books, yet I'm not terribly enthusiastic about their potential outside of non-fiction instructional materials and education. If you want to learn how to change an oil filter in your car or crack an egg open with one hand, an embedded video could be quite valuable. If you're trying to learn a foreign language, interactive audio would be great.

For fiction, however, I think any attempt to add multimedia will likely fail because the magic of fiction is that it happens inside the reader's mind. The sights, sounds and smells within great fiction are much more vivid than reality because fiction happens inside the reader's imagination.

Cheaper E-Reading Devices:
I think we're only 12 months away from some smart e-reading device maker offering readers a free e-reading device in exchange for a monthly subscription plan. For example, I could envision a $9.95/month plan that would entitle the customer to select one book a month from a list, kind of like an ebook of the month club, and then the customer could use the e-reader to discover, sample and purchase other media. I'm really surprised someone hasn't done this yet.

The Future for Writers:
Without a doubt, the opportunities for professional writers to reach readers with their words have never been greater. Most professional writers are sitting on unpublished or reverted-rights works. They should get their content out there asap as an indie ebook, build their catalog, experiment, iterate and start building a modest, long term revenue stream. Getting your work out there is half the battle. Readers will find great content.

(The End)
***

After reading this, I was absolutely sold on the notion that I could not only write a book, but self-publish, distribute,market my book, and make money as well. As Mark had alluded to, I had in fact already a ton of materials that were already completed. As a teacher, and a blogger, I had lots of material which to choose from for my first self-publishing effort.

I prepared my material for Smashwords, yet for some unexplainable reason, I was unable to successfully navigate the system. Whether I failed to fully understand how to format my book, or whether there was some technical malfunction, I will never know. The end result, after a week of trying, was that I was unable to get my book published.

I would persist, and finally succeed, in getting published on Smashwords. However, the initial experience, where I had difficulty in navigating the formatting system, left me with a desire to find another way to self-publish. I wanted to find a place to publish my work that had a system so simple that a person like me, a content creator, but by no means tech savvy, would have no problems.

I kept looking, by now with a clear understanding of what I wanted. Something easy to do, fast, and with no investment required. I was looking for a sure thing, since I had no money.

And then, there it was. I had found it, not on Google or tucked away in the confines of some article, but in plain sight, on YouTube. I found Jason Matthews http://bit.ly/13v8IGw

After watching the video, I became convinced that Jason had broken the code. In other words, he had learned the secrets to self-publishing. After making many expensive mistakes, he had finally found the Holy Grail. The key word, for me, was "FREE".

Since I had no money to invest, "FREE" is the approach I had been looking for. I read his website http://bit.ly/15rfRtq and learned what I think was the most helpful information for me: Createspace https://www.createspace.com/ . You sign up, and then get literally walked through a process step by step, so simple that the few mistakes you make from inexperience do not prevent you from navigating from beginning to end, successfully.

Before we go further, it is important for me to make some disclosures. I am a teacher of English, and I enjoy writing. I am not Stephen King, or Dan Brown, or J.K. Rowling. In other words, what you learn from me is what I have learned in publishing 100 times, how to get from A-Z, from beginning to end, of getting your book published. Making money is what comes with patience.

Anyway, I fulfilled this dream ne hundred times, but I have yet to write a best seller, a Paid Best Seller. I have had an Amazon Kindle FREE Number one. I have had a book picked up as a Hot New Release. Yet a paid number one is not an experience I have had. In sum, I am sharing with you what I have learned, and I hope the story I share with you will be of ultimate benefit to you on your journey to making money, even being an Amazon Number One.

What this chapter has done is set the stage for you to transition from me narrating my experience, to a more direct, actionable path to self-publishing your book. In sum, the dream of becoming a published author was always inside of me, always there, lying under the surface, in my subconscious, waiting for a time to become a dream that I could no longer defer nor deny.

You are reading this book because you have a story to tell, or a book that you want to share with the world. That book is most likely already written, or you would probably be looking at a book dealing with writing, rather than publishing. I am happy to take you on the next stage of your journey, navigating the actual publishing of your book.

When you and I finish, you will be ready for the next stage of your publishing journey, promoting and marketing your book. Yes, it is true what the people say, writing the book is the easy part. Basically, all you have to do is write, and you know how to do that. Yet when the publishing is finished, there is more work to be done.

And if you are like most people, there is no way you just wrote your last book. You will move on to a new project, whether it be fiction or non-fiction, a memoir or a novel, real or imagined. Some of us write because writing is what we do. Without writing, we wouldn't have as much fun as we do. If reading is a journey, then writing is like being the one who takes the journey first, prepares the way, marks the route, and then allows the reader to set off in hopes of discovering the hidden gold, the treasure at the end of the story. As the writer, we already know where the treasure is, and the reader is the element that makes the story complete, magically making everything good. Yes, it is possible to be good again.

Let us look forward then, to what lies ahead. First, we will go to Createspace, and go through the steps, in a guided manner, of what we have to do in order to self-publish. It is a straightforward, direct path, with few difficulties for the inexperienced person to deal with. The time has come to get the paperback book creation process done.

**

Self-Publishing Update: Friday, 13 June 2014

Self-published books' share of the UK market grew by 79% in 2013, with 18m self-published books bought by UK readers last year, according to new statistics.

With print sales falling by 10% last year, and book purchasing as a whole down 4%, ebook sales continue to grow, according to Nielsen's comprehensive tracking of book purchases, up 20% in the UK in 2013, with 80m ebooks bought by UK consumers, to a value of £300m. But it is the DIY market which is showing the most eye-watering growth, up 79% to 18m self-published titles purchased, worth £59m, according to the statistics released on Friday.

Self-published books still account for a tiny proportion of the overall market – 5% of the 323m total books bought, and 3% of the £2185m spent on books last year. But, presenting his figures at The Literary Consultancy's Writing in a Digital Age conference this morning, Steve Bohme, research director at Nielsen Book, predicted the figure was only going to rise.

"Self-publishing is absolutely still booming," he said. "You can see print books down, and ebooks as a whole up – but a lot of that is driven by self-publishing, which has a much higher growth rate."

**

TechCrunch: eBooks Could Finally Edge Past Print in 2018

"Pricewaterhouse Cooper's analysts are predicting (again) that ebooks could soon edge out print as publisher's most lucrative products. What does this mean? Essentially that as ebook popularity and pricing stabilizes, users will spend more on bits than they will on pulp. The resulting switch could be the final nail in the print coffin." – John Biggs, Nov. 23, 2014.

The New York Times created a chart showing rising revenue from e-books, leading to slightly over 50% US penetration in 2018. In the United States and Britain, sales of e-books represent between a quarter and a third of the consumer book market and, by 2018, will edge out printed and audio books as the most lucrative segment, according to projections by the consulting firm PricewaterhouseCoopers.

Mark Coker 2014 Predictions

All authors become indie authors - Back in the dark ages of publishing, you were either traditionally published or weren't published. Writers who couldn't get a publishing deal were seen as failures, because without the access to the publisher's printing press, distribution and professional know-how, it was virtually impossible to reach readers. Today, failure is not an option. The next generation of writers can begin writing their book with the full confidence that one way or another, it will get published. Traditionally published authors now realize they have desirable publishing alternatives they never had before. Once a writer - any writer - comes to the realization that the power in the publishing industry has transfered from publishers to writers, it opens up a new world of possibilities. Publishing no longer becomes an either/or question. The best writers will have the option to publish independently AND traditionally, or do one or the other. It's their choice. Both options are worthy of consideration by all writers, and can be mutually complementary. Even if you're a traditionally published author today, you're an indie author because you decide what happens with your next project.

CHAPTER 5
CREATESPACE AUTHOR SPOTLIGHT

Meet My Publisher: Createspace

In conversation with my wife and inspiration, Gaby.

Publish Your Words, Your Way

That's the motto of CreateSpace, my publisher. In one week, I became a three-time published author:

Teaching Debate in Chile

Teaching Academic Writing

I still can't believe it. If you click on the three links above, like I did, you have to believe it. It's true: I am a published author.

It's a dream come true, really. Maybe that's why the people at CreateSpace say: "**Authors are at the heart of what we do**."

It's that simple.

"Our innovative free tools and top-notch professional services make publishing and distribution easier than ever. Plus it pays to self-publish with CreateSpace. Our royalty structure provides industry-leading economics, putting more in your pocket."

"Just think, manufacturing and shipping is taken care of. Your book remains in-stock, without inventory, made on-demand when customers order. And with an array of options, including our free Interior Reviewer and Cover Creator, together we can create the book you've always wanted. "

Teaching Academic Writing
https://www.createspace.com/3801287

Simple from the Start
Inventory Freedom - Books are printed to meet demand.

Free Tools
Tools like Interior Reviewer and Cover Creator allow you to do-it-yourself easily and with great results.

Professional Services
Choose from our affordable design, editing, and marketing services.

Support
Our dedicated team of professionals is ready to help you throughout the process.

More $$$ for You

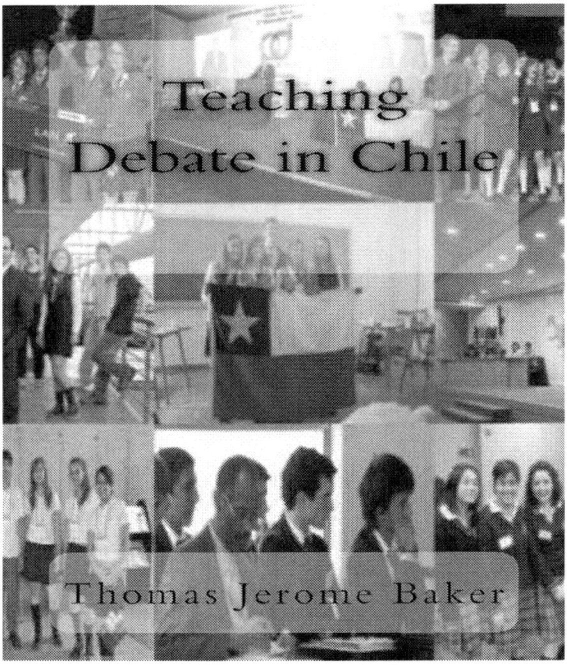

Teaching Debate in Chile
https://www.createspace.com/3784907

Competitive Royalties
Some of the highest royalties in the industry.
Affordable Copies
Low author book prices, regardless of order quantity.

No Setup Fees
Our do-it-yourself option for authors removes hurdles, so you can focus on publishing and distributing.

Library-Quality Books
Professional trade paperback binding ensures a book to be proud of.

Free ISBN
Choose from four ISBN options, including a free CreateSpace-assigned ISBN, when you set up your book.

Celestial Games: The First Pot of Gold
https://www.createspace.com/3785138

Expand Your Reach

Standard Distribution
Free with your membership so you can make your book

available on Amazon.com

On Amazon: http://amzn.to/ZD4I9T

Teaching Debate in Chile
Teaching Academic Writing
Celestial Games: The First Pot of Gold
YouTube Promo Video: Celestial Games
http://bit.ly/11MKeM4

Also, you can sell from your website through a link to your CreateSpace eStore.

Expanded Distribution

Broaden your distribution to online retailers, bookstores, libraries, academic institutions, and distributors within the United States.

***

As you can see, within three weeks, from February 1, 2012 to February 18, 2012, I had self-published three books. Obviously, this feat would have been absolutely impossible with a traditional publisher. No publisher in their right mind would have permitted an unknown author to publish three books, at the same time. At the best, a more cautious approach would have been preferred. Immediately we can begin to see how the new paradigm was going to change, and is changing, the publishing industry.

For me, it was a dream come true (publishing three books), then, and even more so today, with this book being my 60th book, a sort of milestone. As the time has gone by, I've gotten better. For example, nowadays I make my cover before I write the book, reversing the creative process. It is much better for a beginner to do the cover last, after you have defined the contents of the book.

At least it is in the beginning, but as time goes by, you find other ways of working, non-linear. I share this with you now, because it is important for you to know there is no correct order to do things in. You will agree with me, that the main thing is to finish the project.

As for my first three books, they were already written. In total, they had already been downloaded over 20 thousand times. When my books were available for free on my Slideshare account http://bit.ly/11eXrbs I could sometimes just refresh the page and see how the number of downloads and page visits were increasing.

Let me give you another example. My 2012 catalog of books received over 120 thousand views. Thus, you will agree that I had more than enough reason to believe that I should be able to make the transition to self-publishing with a loyal base of readers.

Before moving on, again I admit that I first tried Smashwords, but found the process more daunting and challenging than I could manage. When I finally broke the code, and managed to get a book uploaded to Smashwords, I honestly had no clue as to how I had completed the task.

Here is my profile on Smashwords: https://www.smashwords.com/profile/view/profesorbaker You will note that I have had this profile since February 21, 2012. That is three weeks after I began searching for how to publish my books, which were already written, but unpublished.

Here is a notice I received, dated March 24, 2012, letting me know that I had actually made a sale on Smashwords: Smashwords Purchase Notification: The Professional Learning Network

http://amzn.to/11rHcKr

Dear Thomas,

Per your request, we're writing to notify you someone has purchased your book:

Title: The PLN: Professional Learning Network
Qty: 1
List Price: $0.99
Coupon: None
Price Paid: $0.99
Gift Discount: $0.00
Proceeds: $0.56
Total items: 1
Total proceeds: $0.56
Time: 2012-03-24 06:35:30 PT
Transaction id: 6Y50962065326932L

Sincerely,

The Smashwords Team,
http://www.smashwords.com
https://www.smashwords.com/books/view/136437

Book Description: http://amzn.to/11rHcKr

I am grateful and thankful for all the informal and formal learning opportunities I have had access to through the individual and collective members of my PLN, my Professional Learning Network. Each one of you is indispensable to my learning, and thusly, I treasure all of you, equally. Thank you.

Thanks to the 1,980 members of my LinkedIn network. Through you, I have access to the collective wisdom and knowledge of 12,614,973 people. Let me spell that out: Twelve million, six hundred fourteen thousand, nine hundred and seventy three people. That's an awful lot of people to have in a PLN.

Thanks to my Facebook PLN, all 1,985 of you. Yes, Facebook as a PLN. You guys have shared an awful lot of great information with me about education, learning, and teaching. You've shared links, videos, conferences, seminars, training opportunities, and current news, for all this,Facebook is the place to look.

Twitter, what can I say about you? There are 1,892 of you. One thousand, eight hundred and ninety two. Twitter takes persistence when you first begin. No matter how much info you have about Twitter, the early days are difficult, if you're like most people. But if you're really keen on being current, up to date, on the cutting edge of what's new in your profession and in the world, then you must learn to use Twitter.

Let me be brutally honest: as a PLN, LinkedIn is fantastic, Facebook is spectacular, both are most magnificent social media tools, but they are not Twitter. Twitter is the social media I turn to most often. Having said that, again, all three, Twitter, Facebook, and LinkedIn complement each other well, providing me with an iron triangle of knowledge and news.

Thank you, to all the members of my Professional Learning Network. My learning never stops, http://amzn.to/11rHcKr !

***

I have taken the time to share the info about my experience with Smashwords because they are a very real and viable option for authors. As you can see, for a book priced at $0.99 cents, approximately 2/3 (two thirds) was going to the author. That would be unheard of in a traditional publishing context, and I knew it.

So, let me be perfectly clear, I recommend Smashwords http://www.smashwords.com for authors looking to maximise their profits by publishing their books simultaneously at different publishers. The exposure to potential readers is higher, and obviously the chance is that you will receive higher overall profits.

Having said all that, why didn't I follow this model? The answer is that I decided to committ fully, 100%, to the Amazon Kindle KDP program. I stress quickly that it was a personal decision, as I knew that I had a large amount of material already from which to publish a large number of books from.

Previously I devoted time to show, rather than tell, the benefits open to the authors who choose to participate in the Amazon KDP program. Personally, it suits me fine, and I have been content to have a continuous 100% presence there. In short, the Amazon Kindle KDP is the biggest player, and I have been successful in this way. This economic model benefitted me personally, yet each author needs to decide for themselves what they will do, enroll in the KDP or not.

I will also devote one chapter to how I am able to have a continual, almost unlimited supply of material from which to publish more books on. The answer is an obvious one, since I am continually working through ideas through writing on my blogs. I write often, usually every day, as writing has become almost like breathing, eating, sleeping. I have to write every day, without it I feel out of sync. It does not matter if it is only a little, or a lot. In my case, I live to write, and I write to live.

Now we are ready to go through the steps of what we can understand as, "Uploading a Book" to Createspace. Uploading a book is a synonym for self-publishing, and basically, it is as simple as uploading a Word document to my Slideshare account to be shared for free. As I think of this, I must admit that it was good training for the upload process at CreateSpace.

Yet, the difference is that now it is an actual book. It comes with an ISBN, with a price, with royalty payments, with everything that makes an author, an author. As the singer Jessie J. would say, we're talking about money, because there is a price tag attached.

In the next chapter, it is time to "school" ourselves. What is the sequence of steps necessary to upload a book to CreateSpace. We will go through the process, giving the actual basic steps needed to publish our work. By the time we finish, you will be able to publish any book you have written.

**

CHAPTER 6
UPLOADING YOUR BOOK TO CREATESPACE: A STEP BY STEP GUIDE

Step 1:
Go to the Createspace website, here https://www.createspace.com/ . Click on the link.

Step 2:
Log In if you already have an account, or Sign Up if it is your first time here. Once you are logged in, you will see another page. Here you will need to click "Add New Title" which is located on the upper left hand side of the screen in the box labelled, "My Account."

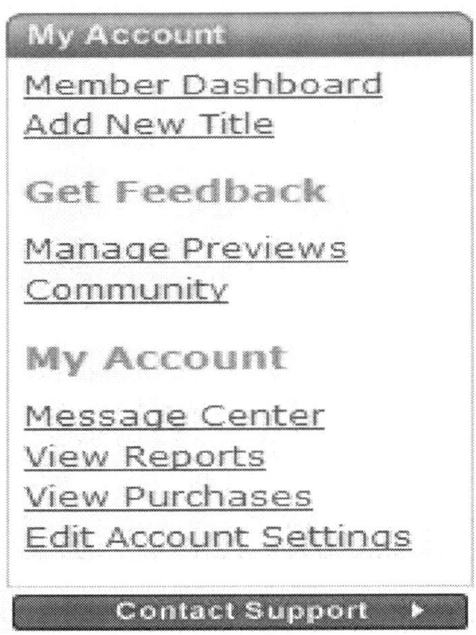

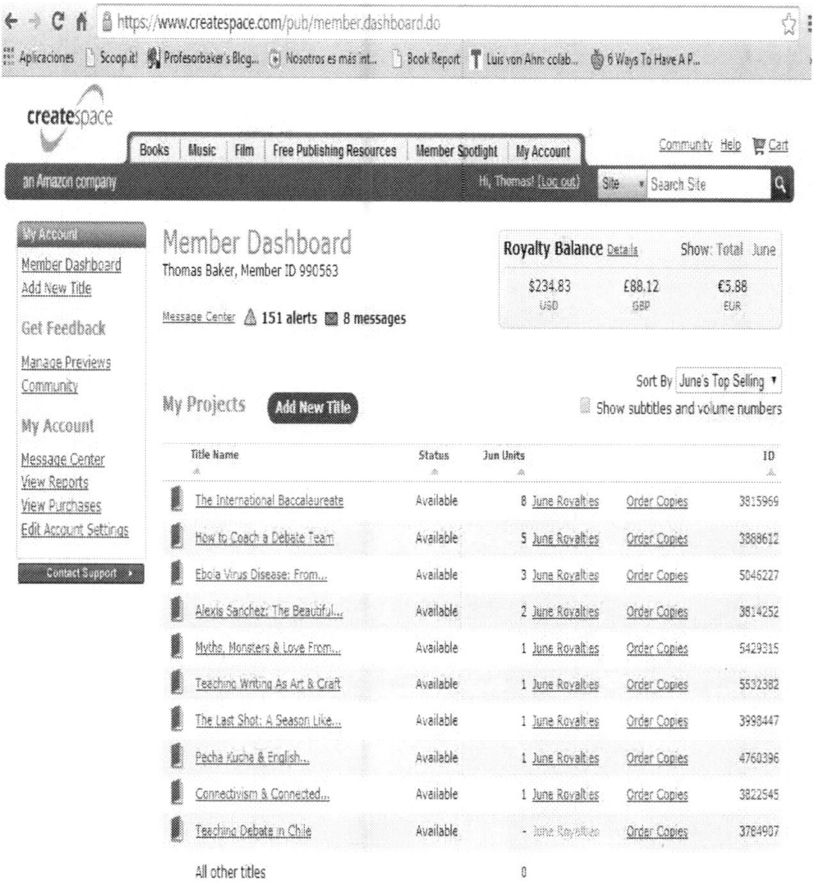

Step 3:

On the **Start Your New Project** page, fill in the name of your book, the type of project and choose a setup method. There are two choices:

Guided: A step-by-step process with directions along the way. (I always choose this because I'd never remember the steps.)

Expert: A streamlined single-page experience for those familiar with the process.

Click the **Get Started** button by your choice and move on to the next step.

Step 4:

Title Information page: Fill in your book title, subtitle (if applicable), author name, contributors, series name and number (if applicable) and other details.

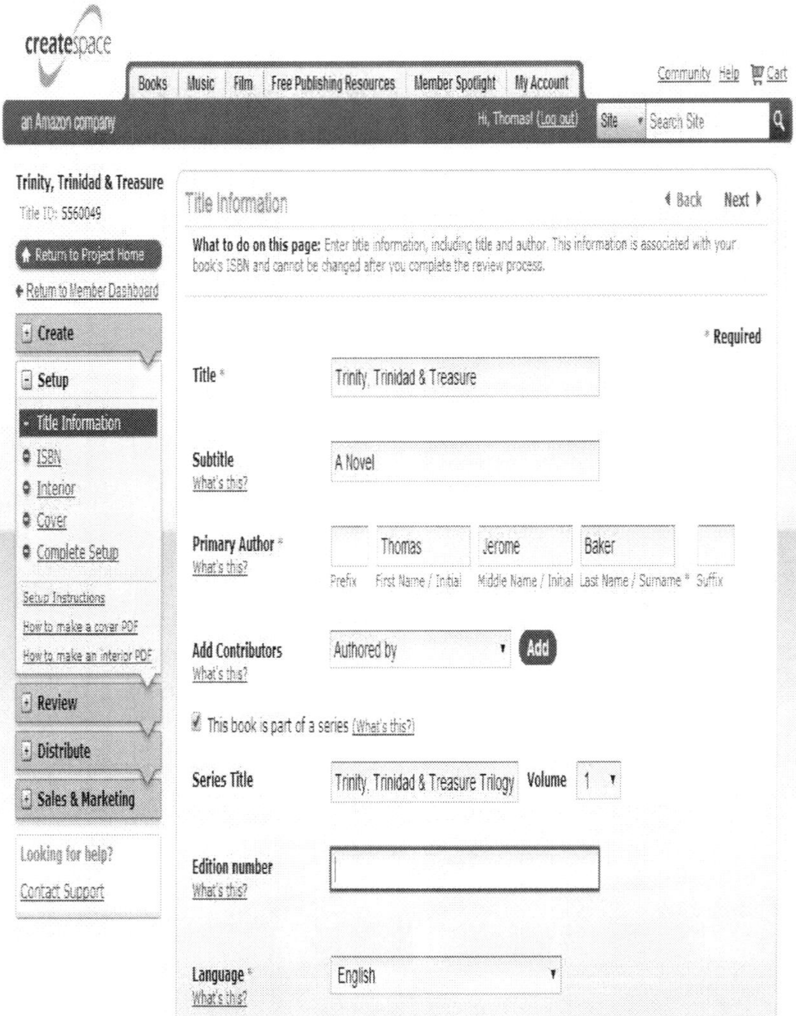

Note: If you leave **Publication Date** blank, the date your book publishes on Createspace will be added. If you published the book previously, on Kindle for instance or with a traditional publisher, you can fill in the original pub date if you wish.

Click **Save & Continue**.

Step 5: ISBN

CreateSpace says, "An ISBN (number) is required to publish and distribute a book." They offer four options. One is free.

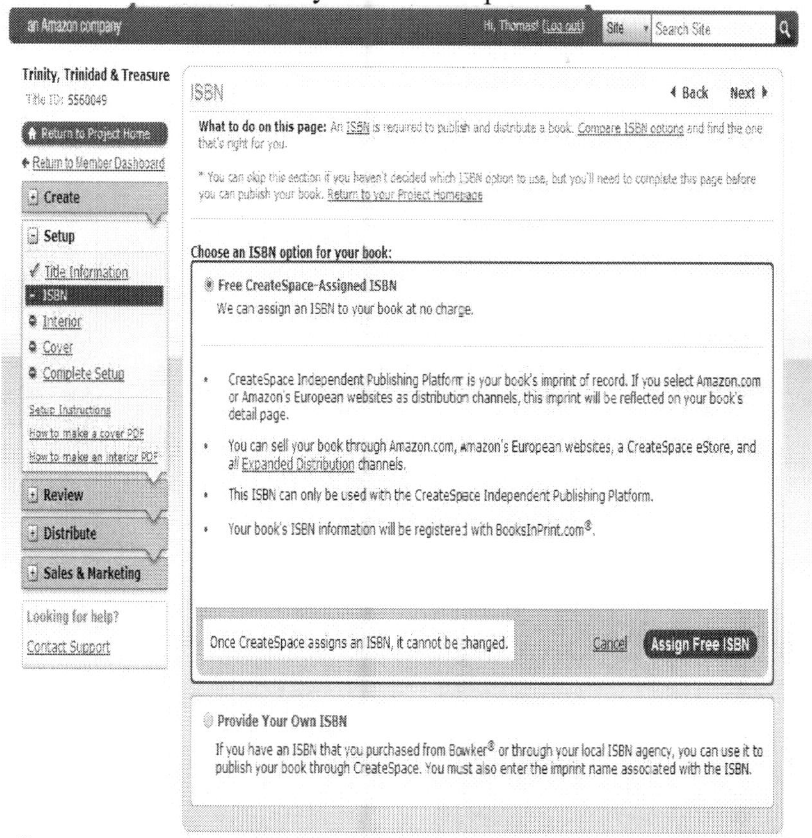

Note: Compare the options carefully because once you make your choice it cannot be changed. Choose and click **Continue**.

Step 6: Interior

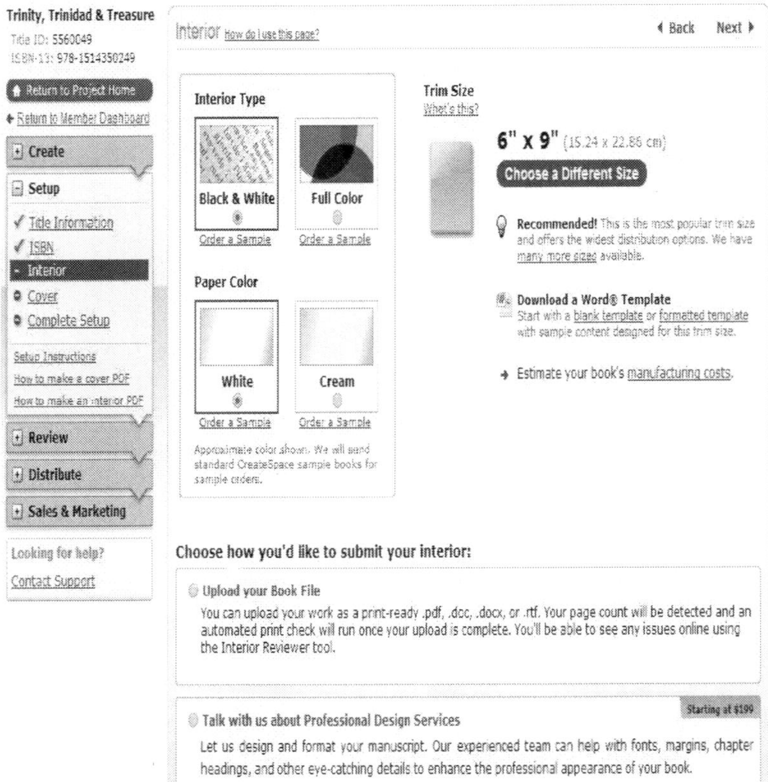

Choose from:

- black & white or color
- paper color (white or cream)
- trim size (size of your book). The most popular trim size is 6" x 9" – trade paperback size. Createspace does not offer standard paperback size.

Next comes the "fun" part, uploading your book!

You can either hire a Createspace professional to do it for you, with prices starting at $349, or you can do it yourself.

Do it yourself methods:

1. Upload your work as a print-ready .pdf, .doc, .docx, or .rtf file.

2. Download a Word® Template, either a blank template or a formatted template with sample content designed for the trim size you choose. I use the formatted 6" x 9" template.

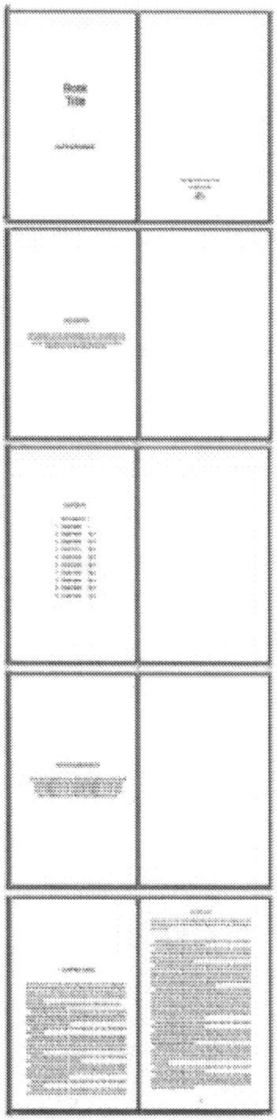

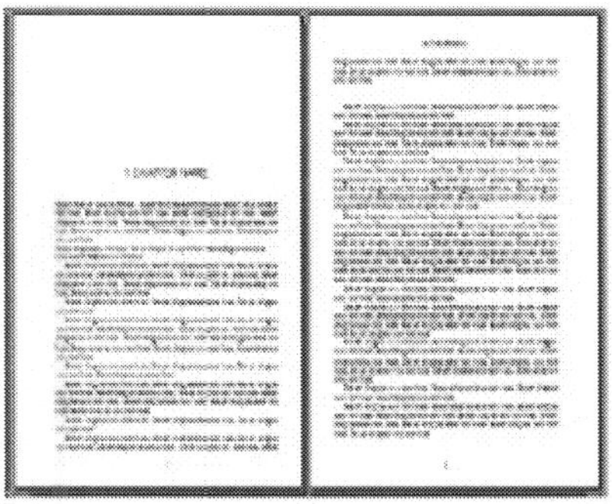

The thumbnails on the left show how a Createspace formatted template is set up. Each pair of pages represents the front and back sides of one printed page. The left page of each pair would actually be the right hand page in a book, while the right one would be on the left (backside of right page.)

The midline in each pair represents the outside edge of the page; the left and right borders are the edge of the page that would be bound, forming the book's spine. Because more space is necessary on the bound edge, the text must be offset closer to the outside edge (the center line of each pair.) See this spacing difference in the illustration above.

There is a table of contents included in the formatted template. If you don't want one in your book, simply delete that pair of pages. You can also delete the dedication and acknowledgements pages if you wish, or you can add pages to the front matter, such as a list of your published books and/or "Praise for" pages with short review excerpts. I place this type of material before the title page as do traditional publishers.

TIP: Use section breaks between the elements of your front matter to maintain proper spacing. This also allows you to add page numbers when you come to the body of your story. If you want page numbers in the front matter, use Roman numerals.

Add alternating headers, placing your book title on the right hand pages and your author name on the left.

Regarding font styles, the CreateSpace conversion program doesn't recognize all fonts, so it's best to stick to standard ones unless you want to have problems.

I use Times New Roman 12 point for body text, varying sizes for chapter headings and in the front matter. Bold and italics are okay. Be careful to check your font for headers. I got in trouble once when an odd font snuck by me in a header. The Createspace program didn't like it!

After you upload your formatted manuscript and it goes through the Createspace automated print check, view your book page by page using the Interior Reviewer.

If Createspace catches formatting errors, you will need to fix them and re-upload. This can be time consuming, but you want your baby to look good, right? In case you can't figure out the glitch, email or call CreateSpace Support. Their people helped me through a couple roadblocks when I set up my first book for print.

7. Cover:
Choose a finish for your book cover, either matte or glossy. This is new. Until recently, all covers were glossy.

Next, choose how to submit your book cover. There are three methods:

Build Your Cover Online with Cover Creator, a free Createspace tool to design your book covers. (See #7 below)

Professional Cover Design, starting at $399.

Upload a Print-Ready PDF Cover: Createspace provides detailed instructions for this method.

8. Using **Cover Creator:** Choose from several pages of pre-made Createspace cover designs (below on left) or design your own cover using a blank template (on right.)

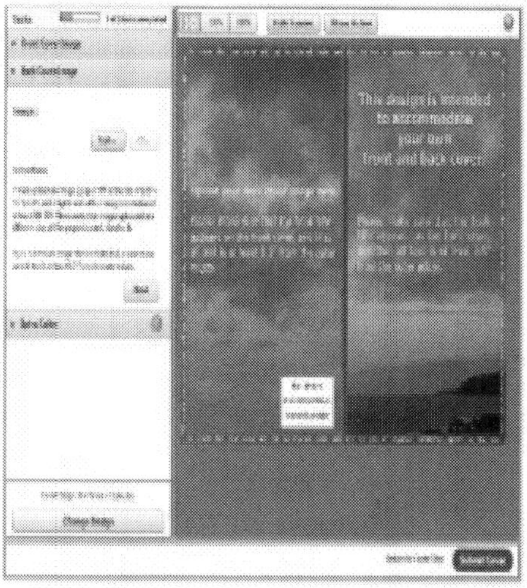

Above: This is the template I use.

First, design the front cover (I do this offline) making sure your image has a DPI of at least 300. Anything less than that will be rejected by the Createspace program.

After the front cover successfully loads, design the back cover. Include:

a short, catchy blurb

short review excerpts

an author photo if you wish

Look at the back of paperback books for ideas, and be careful to leave space for the barcode and trimming, as per Createspace instructions.

Lastly, set up the spine.

9. Complete Setup: Review your project setup. If everything looks okay, submit your files for review. You can go back and make changes if you need to. When ready, submit for review.

10. Review: The CreateSpace automated review program makes sure your work passes muster for "manufacturing and cataloging". If it does, you will be asked if you want to order a proof copy (at cost) for your final approval. I always do this because there could still be issues that need correcting. When you are satisfied, give Createspace the go-ahead to publish your print book.

Note: Do the following while waiting for the automated review to be completed (it may take several hours or longer). Note, you will also receive an email from CreateSpace, stating the results of the automated check process. Here is an example of the email I received for this book:

Dear Thomas,

Your interior file for ***How To Self-Publish Your Book For Free*** (Title ID: 4307162) has gone through our automated checks. We found **2 issue(s)** that you should review before proceeding with your title setup.

Review your interior file online
Get more information on the issues we found
See useful trim guides and print margins
Check for typos, grammar, and formatting problems

Once you understand these issues:
Make changes to address the issues in your file
Upload your revised file
Address any remaining issues found through our automated checks

Get help solving these issues:
Our Free Publishing Resources has tips on dealing with common formatting mistakes. Ask specific formatting questions and get answers in our Community. You can also purchase professional support for PDF files with our Supported Interior PDF service or give your book a professional layout with one of our design services.

Sincerely,
The CreateSpace Team

11. Distribution Channels: Choose distribution channels. Expanded Distribution used to cost $25 but is now FREE!

12. Pricing: Set a price for your book. Use the built in calculator to determine what the royalties will be. Keep in mind that distributors usually discount the book price and Amazon will match the discounted price. If you set your price too low, you proceeds will suffer when the book is discounted. Of course you don't want to price your book so high that it scares off readers.

13. Description: Provide a description for your sales page. Assign a BISAC Category; add your author bio; set language, country of publication; choose search keywords; check for adult content if applicable and if you want large print.

In conclusion, take your time, follow directions on the site and, if you ever get stuck, contact Createspace support. Their people are courteous and helpful.

**

As you can see, the process is very thorough. Repeat these steps, uploading the manuscript, checking the interior file, until you have completed this step and are content with the document that will become your books interior file.

You can now go on to the Cover Step. This is an area in which CreateSpace has provided a large variety of attractive covers to choose from. The cover preparation is step by step, intuitive, guided by the "Cover Maker" program.

It is free, and costs nothing, and produces covers that are as imaginative as the authors are. There are many who argue, convincingly, that a cover is so important that you should consider making an investment, and paying someone who is experienced to make your cover. I can only tell you my experience, and let you decide what to do.

After going through all of the creative process, of writing, and uploading, I wanted to stay actively in control of my finished product. Therefore, I looked at the covers available, one by one, trying several, before I reached my conclusion about which one to use.

As I have said before, I had no money to invest, and given the experience I have gained, would advise anyone reasonably creative to try to design your own cover.

For me, it is important to be able to say, when the book comes out, that I personally had a hand in everything. I wrote the book, uploaded it, and designed the cover. If the book flops, and fails to make money, then the person responsible for that is the man staring at me in the mirror, me!

I have no one to blame but myself, and therefore will make the effort to understand what it takes to make a better cover.

I am not above taking a risk, to see how it works out. I know that I can change covers, experiment with designs, until I find one that is having success, and selling books. This is an area in which patience, rational thought, and observation of what effects a little change has on the outcome of sales.

Let me sum this up. I make and design my own covers. I use the Cover Creator Software provided by CreateSpace. It prompts me through the cover design stage step by step. There is little need for me to show screen shots, because it is well designed.

Finally, you are ready to complete the setup when you are satisfied with your cover.

Again, I repeat, that this is an area that is a matter of personal taste, and open to your creativity. There are people who pay people who are experienced cover crators to make and design professional looking covers.

If you have written a novel, for example, and look at some of the covers that the novels have, you begin to get a feeling that investing $5 or $10 dollars might be much cheaper, and much more beneficial in increasing the sales volume of your book.

On the other hand, if you are writing nonfiction, it is highly likely that a good camera is all you need to take an outstanding picture that you can use for your cover.

CHAPTER 7
PROOF YOUR BOOK

Dear Thomas,

Your interior file for ***How To Self-Publish Your Book For Free on CreateSpace & Kindle*** (Title ID: 4307162) has gone through our automated checks. We found **1 issue(s)** that you should review before proceeding with your title setup.

**

The issue at this point relates to the quality of a photo I am using. After I determine whether or not this is relevant in terms of quality of the photo, I decide to continue. The next step at this point is to complete the setup and then wait 24 – 48 hours for the files to be checked.

Living in Chile, at the ends of the Earth, literally, this final review of the files I have submitted usually take no more than 24 hours. It is rare for the review process to exceed this 24 hour period. What I am waiting on is a message that says my files are printable. Here is an example below:

**

Congratulations your files are printable!
We've reviewed the interior and cover files for Selected Essays on Education, #4291732 and they meet submission requirements.

The next step in the publishing process is to **proof your book**:

FOLLOW THIS LINK TO GET STARTED:

****

https://tsw.createspace.com/title/xxxxxxxxxxxxx

****

Our reviewers did find some non-blocking issues with your files. Some of these issues may have been fixed causing alterations to your files.

We have noticed that you have left the ISBN information blank in your interior file. As a courtesy, we have added your title?s ISBN information to your file. To determine if you?re satisfied with this change, we recommend reviewing a proof of your title

Best regards,
The CreateSpace Team

Please direct questions to our Member Support team at:

https://www.createspace.com/Member/Support.do

Visit our informative member-driven Community for additional questions at:

https://www.createspace.com/en/community/index.jspa

**

What tasks do I have to do to proof my book? First, I click on the link provided in the email where it says:

FOLLOW THIS LINK TO GET STARTED:

****
https://tsw.createspace.com/title/xxxxxxxxxxxxx

****

I click on the link and then I see this:

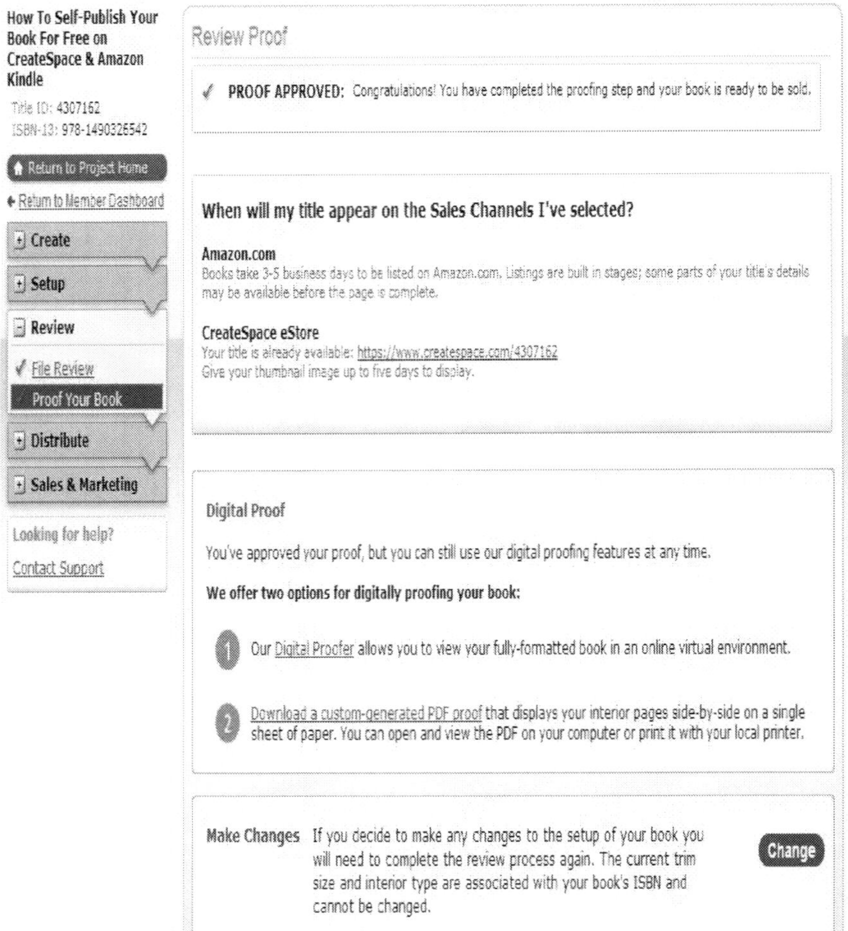

I am using the digital proofer. I have two options:

1. The digital, online proofer, and
2. Downloading a custom-generated PDF proof.

I recomend using both. Again, go over the proof several times, looking for general layout problems first, and then for details such as grammar, spelling, punctuation.

If there is a problem, correct it in your file, upload the corrected file, and repeat the process.

If there is no problem, approve the proof.

After the proof is approved, you will see this message shown below. At the top of the screen will be a green check mark that says, "PROOF APPROVED." At the bottom of the screen will be a blue field that says, "CONTINUE TO SALES CHANNEL."

Congratulations! You just published your book.

The remaining details have to deal with sales channels and pricing. For beginners, it is best to build up a base of loyal readers by selling your books cheap, as a general rule. However, that does not mean it is impossible to charge a higher price, and simply wait to find out if your books will manage to sell at a higher price.

Add in the remaining info about the book description when asked, and within 24 hours your book will be available for sale worldwide! You are a self-published author now!

Again, congratulations!

Savor the moment, enjoy it, and then get ready for the next phase of the book, marketing and promotion.

If you elect to put out a Kindle version of your book, CreateSpace will provide your book cover and book file to Amazon Kindle for upload. At Amazon, you follow a simple, intuitive, user-friendly program that uploads your file.

Within 24 hours, you will receive a message from Amazon:

**

Hello from Amazon KDP!

The book "Selected Essays on Education: Call & Response -

"When One Teaches Two Learn"" you recently submitted to KDP and enrolled in KDP Select has been published to the Kindle Store and is already available* for readers to purchase here.

KDP Select allows you to enjoy benefits, such as earning a share of a monthly fund when readers borrow your book from the Kindle Owners' Lending Library and a promotional opportunity to offer your book as free to readers for up to 5 days every 90 days to expand your reach.

For more details on KDP Select, check out this page.

You can check on the current month's KDP Select fund by visiting your Bookshelf.

Also, you can find your book's number of borrows in real time through your Month-to-Date Unit Sales report here.

Now that your KDP Select-enrolled book is live, you can manage its free promotion days in your Bookshelf by clicking the "Manage Promotions" link from the "Actions" menu or from the "Edit book details" page.

Your book's initial enrollment in KDP Select lasts for 90 days. For your convenience, your book's enrollment will be automatically renewed for another 90 days, unless you cancel automatic renewal by un-checking "Automatically renew this book's enrollment in KDP Select for another 90 days" box under "Enrollment Details" of your book before your book's current enrollment term expires.

***

You are finished. Together, we have completed our mission. We set out to self-publish your book for free on CreateSpace and Amazon Kindle. That is what we have achieved. I have supplied the knowledge, the encouragement, and the belief in your ability to teach yourself everything you needed to know.

You have done that, and will now move on to the fulfillment of your dreams. To make your dream come true, to make money creating and publishing eBooks on CreateSpace and Kindle, you have a lot of hard work ahead of you.

You must continue to learn, to teach yourself what is the best way to attract customers, what is the best way to price your book, whether or not to change small details, such as cover, title, blurb, photos or no photos, and free promotions if you are enrolled in the Amazon KDP program.

What is most likely is that the last part of your goal, making money, will happen for you, if you are patient. No matter how much time this goal requires, no matter how steep the learning curve, it is now a matter of perseverance, and diligently teaching yourself each detail necessary to advance towards your money making goals.

Experience says that most of us writers will go this way, gaining success in small increments, as time passes. For the truly exceptional cases, your book just might be the next "Hunger Games", the next "DaVinci Code". You won't know until you try!

I would like to thank you for going on this journey with me. It has been an enjoyable one for me, and a productive one for you. You have taken steps to achieve your goals, to self-publish, on CreateSpace & Kindle. You are closer than never before to making money. You have made your book available, and that was fundamental in your plans. It is now a matter of time.

Thank you for reading this book. Thank you for placing your trust in me to help you achieve your goals. I appreciate your faith in me, and I have no doubt that you will go far. I salute you, as a CreateSpace publisher, as a Kindle publisher. I wish you nothing but the very best, and if there is ever any question you have for me, something in this book that was not clear, or puzzling in any way, please feel free to contact me.

I will respond to your email, to any social media in which you contact me. Most importantly, count me as a member of your team, from this day forward. Your success will always be something I am deeply interested in, and willing to help, in any way that is feasible to me.

Finally, before we say goodbye for now, I have one final request for you. Thank you, again for buying this book. Since you have bought this book, Amazon will allow you to write a review of this book on Amazon. That's right, if you bought this book, rather than getting a free copy, Amazon will permit you to share your review with other people who might be considering buying this book.

Will you please write a review of this book if you are happy with the book? Your review will be helpful, and I give you my thanks in advance. I sincerely appreciate your support.

If there is anything in this book that you did not like, or did not find useful or helpful, then I ask you to please contact me, at my personal email, and let me know about it.

I promise you I will do everything in my power to address the issue in a way that shows respect for your your views. If you write a bad review, it would mean that I have no chance to contact you to address the issue. As you know, there are many possibilities open to correct issues that you are concerned about. Writing a negative review, giving a low rating, is difficult for writer to overcome after the fact. I have done my best to create value for you. If I failed, again, please give me the opportunity to improve.

Finally, I thank you for everything, for buying the book, for reading it and using it. I thank you for your future contact, with good news about the success you are having and the money you are making. We both know the road to success is not one that happens to come to an end overnight, but steady progress brings everyone, sooner or later, to the destiny and the destination they have set their aim to achieve.

May God Bless You,

TEN TIPS FOR USING CREATESPACE

1. Plan your book.
2. Get your information together before you start.
3. Pick a category.
4. Decide on keywords.
5. Decide on price.
6. Choose industry standard size for your book.
7. Format your book properly.
8. Get an amazing cover.
9. Use images at least 300 dpi.
10. Submit your file.

As I look at the ten tips above, I will admit that I have broken all of the above rules. Guilty as charged, I am. For me, self-publishing was, is, and always will be, difficult. It's not easy even when you have published over a hundred books. We simply have to keep learning and improving our books as we learn what works.

For this book, now my second edition, I have revised, re-edited, and re-published. The book is better than it was before, and it costs less also. I'm using an attractive, new cover image. I like the way this book represents the knowledge I have gained about how to publish for free on Amazon Kindle and CreateSpace.

The book is storytelling and it is craft. Why and how this book came to be what it is, is a story of my journey from wishful thinking to making my publishing dream a reality. My story adds value to the book because you get more than just a set of instructions about how to publish a book. You. Get. Much. More.

You get a conversation about self-publishing that is human. It is trial and it is error. It is pride and it is humility. It is success and it is failure. This is the story of my publishing journey, and it has produced an immense amount of satisfaction for me. I have no doubt it will do the same for you. So, don't be afraid to experiment, and above all, have fun. Enjoy your journey...

AUTHOR INTERVIEW:

THOMAS JEROME BAKER

1 - **How long have you been writing?**

Thomas Jerome Baker: About 30 years, so let me explain myself. My first book was self-published two years ago. My first bit of creative writing came when I was in 9th grade. My teacher, Mrs. Kelly, asked the class one day to write a story. I remember thinking to myself that I could do it. I sat for a moment or two, quietly thinking of a story. For some reason, the 6 Million Dollar Man came to mind.

So, my story was a science fiction piece about a man who needed to plug himself into a wall socket to charge his super powers up. I think I called it "Electric Man, Where the Charge is on You". Mrs. Kelly gave me an A on the short story and I laid my pen to rest.

It wasn't until many years later, here in Chile, when I began to write stories for my students to read. I needed to motivate the boys at my school, Colegio del Verbo Divino, 13-14 years old, to engage with reading, and I figured the best way to do it would be by writing stories which were clearly about them. "Meet Me in Memphis", Looking For Catarina, and the scifi thriller, "Boudicca, Her-Story" were soon written in short order. The stories were dormant inside of me, just waiting for a reason to be written. That was two years ago, when I first got them published and out to the world on Amazon Kindle.

2 - **What inspired you to start?**

TJB: The start was definitely connected to the paradigm shift we are experiencing in publishing right now. Writing a book, any book, is actually the easy part, but getting published is a tedious process. The only thing the writer controls is the writing, everything else is guided externally. For me, the freedom to write, and then subject the writing to actual readers, who decide with their wallets if something I've written is good or not, is extremely satisfying. The role of gatekeeper, if you will, is where it ought to be, with the consumer, the reader of our work.

3 - **Do you remember your first piece of writing? If yes, what was it about?**

TJB: Does a love note count as a piece of writing? If it does, the first piece of purposeful writing I remember, even before "Electric Man", goes way back, to fourth grade, when I was head over heels infatuated with a very pretty girl named Brenda. I wrote her a card one day which said something like this: I love you. Do you love me? Yes or No? (Circle one) The letter came back clearly marked, "No". It was then that I decided that I needed to learn how to express myself in writing as well as I could speaking!

4 - **What are your favorite stories to write?**

TJB: I love my profession, teaching English as a Foreign Language. My stories are experiential based, in which I try to shed some light on a topic by looking at it through the lens of my own experience, and then connecting the dots between theory and practice, in much the same way as a storyteller does.

5 - **What are the benefits of being a writer?**

TJB: Well, it's not the money, because writers don't make a lot of money, at least, not at first anyway. With time, the financial rewards do begin to show up, and that is of course gratifying. As a teacher however, I firmly believe it helps me to connect with the problems that students have when they are writing, because I experience the same problems. How to deal with a blank sheet of paper is a common problem, for instance. The aesthetic benefit of writing, however, when all is said and done, is that writers leave a legacy behind. Whatever you write lives forever, and that is quite profound, the idea of being able to communicate with future generations of readers that are as of yet unborn.

6 - Who is your favorite author? Why?

Robert Louis Stevenson
Treasure Island, *Kidnapped*, *Strange Case of Dr Jekyll and Mr Hyde*.

TJB: Robert Louis Stevenson. He wrote books like Treasure Island and Dr. Jekyl and Mr. Hyde which have been favorites of mine since I first read them so many years ago. My teachers in elementary school used to actually give me books to read during the summer holidays, and that is how I got my own copy of Treasure Island. His writing style is very attractive, not only to me, but to other great writers as well. Stevenson achieved literary fame during his lifetime, when this was an honor reserved for only a very select group of writers. Here is what we find out about him from Wikipedia:

> "A literary celebrity during his lifetime, Stevenson now ranks among the 26 most translated authors in the world.[3] His works have been admired by many other writers, including Borges, Brecht, Sir Arthur Conan Doyle, Pavese, Hemingway, Kipling, Jack London, Nabokov, and G. K. Chesterton."

This is a man who was admired by writers who each are equally great, if not greater, in their own literary accomplishments. That obviously says a lot about the ability of Stevenson as a writer. For me, what I especially like about him is the way he uses the personal essay to engage the reader with a voice that makes you feel comfortable with him.

I take this as a point of departure in my previous book, “Selected Essays on Education”, and to a certain extent in this one. As you know, this style follows a rich, 400 year old literary tradition of the personal essay. For me, it’s the presence of the human voice, and I find it to be the way I’m most comfortable writing. So naturally I gravitate towards Stevenson, who favored this particular way of literary expression.

7 - What has been your favorite book to write and why?

TJB: For me, the current book, is always going to be the favorite book, the one I like most, because my writing process is one of crafting a story that is plausible for me, on a number of different levels. If the story does this, has credibility, whether fictional or non-fiction, then I am content that I’ve been able to tell the story that I wanted to tell.

In other words, my first aim is to please myself, and when I accomplish that, I then ask the reader to also enjoy the story I have told, (to come along with me), in the dialogic sense of Call and Response, with the Call being me saying, “Here’s a story I like, what do you think?” The Response then is the reader, affirming or not their enjoyment of the story.

8 - What book are you working on now? And when is it available for purchase?

TJB: I just released “Selected Essays on Education: Call & Response – “When One Teaches Two Learn”. It came out on the 27th of May, and I’m content with the essays it includes because the unifying notion is one of Call and Response, whether in song, in writing, or in speech, relating back to culture and taking on some heavy issues such as the Islamic inventions in the supposed “Dark Ages”.

I believe many readers will find it interesting and entertaining at the same time, while being absolutely respectful towards Islam, the traditions and beliefs. For instance, the period of time we know as the Dark Ages is actually considered to be the Golden Ages, as there was a robust time frame in which Islams greatest thinkers and inventors were coming up with inventions and innovations on a rather continuous recurring basis.

Islams great inventor is a man named Al-Jazari http://bit.ly/17h7fZV . He is a fascinating wealth of ancient knowledge which very little is known in the western world, although Al-Jazari published extensively. It makes you curious to know more about Al-Jazari and the Golden Ages, when Europe was going through the Dark Ages.

http://amzn.to/1cTYt8L

9 - **Outside of writing what do you like to do?**

TJB: I enjoy reading, which is obvious, being a writer. Fiction, non-fiction, I read almost anything I can get my hands on. I've always enjoyed a wide diversity of reading material, and that has been helpful for me in developing my skills as a writer. I'm a linguist, being trilingual.

Besides English, I speak Spanish and German, and I enjoy reading works in the original language of its authors. I also enjoy living as an expat in Chile, which is a very beautiful country, unrivaled in its diversity.

Chile has the driest desert in the world (the Atacama) in the north and the coldest region in the world in the south, the Antarctic. In between there are beaches and mountains, vineyards and forests, countryside and sprawling cities. To this, add the Chilean cuisine, a hearty South American food, the land, the culture, the traditions and the people, who never cease to amaze me, even after 12 years living here. In sum, my favorite thing to do is to get to know as much of this wonderful country as I can!

10 - **In one sentence describe your art, your personal writing style.**

TJB: This one is going to be hard to do. Here goes:

My personal writing style is dialogic, one in which I try to make the reader feel at ease with me, and to Respond to the Call of my authorial voice, a literary Call & Response, based on my lived reality.

11 - **Is there anything else you would like us to know?**

TJB: A good friend once told me, "Write what you know about, and you will always have plenty to write about." I sincerely feel that experiential writing, at its core, allows me to be introspective, to slow the world down, to reflect, and then to share whatever bit of wisdom I have discovered, no matter how small or insignificant it may seem. In this way, I have truly given an adequate Response to the Call of the reader to share something personal, something that really matters, because its important somehow. In turn, I am thankful for the readers who have read the experiential books I write, because it's the essence of what I do as a writer, namely share my experience. http://www.amazon.com/dp/B00D1DY6BC

B) Can you give us a short bio, two or three paragraphs?

Biography

Thomas Baker is the Past-President of TESOL Chile (2010-2011). He is the Head of the English Department at Colegio Dunalastair in Chicureo, (20 km outside of Santiago, Chile).

He is the Co-Founder and Co-Organiser of EdCamp Santiago 2012 & Edcamp Chile 2013, free, participant-driven, democratic, conversation based professional development for teachers, by teachers. EdCamp Santiago 2012 was held at Universidad Mayor in Santiago.

Thomas is also a Past Member of the Advisory Board for the International Higher Education Teaching and Learning Association (HETL), where he also serves as a reviewer and as the HETL Ambassador for Chile.

Thomas enjoys writing about a wide variety of topics. Thus far, he has written the following genres: romance, historical fiction, autobiographical, sports history/biography, and English Language Teaching. He has published a total of sixty (60) books.

The source and inspiration for his writing comes from his family, his wife Gabriela, and his son, Thomas Jerome Baker, Jr.

C) Can you share 1-2 jpg of your book covers?

https://www.createspace.com/3823252

D) A profile picture of yourself

E) Links to your FB fan page, website, Twitter, etc..

Facebook: http://facebook.com/profesorbaker

Website: http://profesorbaker.com/

Twitter: @profesortbaker https://twitter.com/profesortbaker

Amazon: http://www.amazon.com/Thomas-Jerome-Baker/e/B007G9HJFM

ABOUT THE AUTHOR

Thomas Jerome Baker is the Past-President of TESOL Chile (2010–2011) . He is the Past-Coordinator of the English Department at SEK International High School in Santiago, Chile.

Thomas is also a member of the "Comunidad de Innovación Escolar" (School Innovation Community), sponsored jointly by the Education 2020 Foundation and the Telefónica Foundation. He is a past member of the Advisory Board for the International Higher Education Teaching and Learning Association (HETL), where he also serves as a reviewer and as the HETL Ambassador for Chile.

Thomas enjoys writing about a wide variety of topics. His writing ranges from historical fiction to romance, from the autobiographical to the biographical, from English Language Teaching (ELT) to the wider field of educational leadership and evaluation.

"Selected Essays on Education" is his 59th book, all self-published, and available on Amazon http://amzn.to/PCX6ho . If you have read and enjoyed any of his books, please take the time to write a positive customer review.

Thank you, dear reader(s), in advance, for your time, your support and your generosity...

Connect with Thomas

Thank you so much for taking the time to read this book. I hope you have enjoyed reading it as much as I enjoyed putting it together for you.

If you have any questions of any kind, feel free to contact me directly at my email: profesorbaker@gmail.com

You can follow me on Twitter: https://twitter.com/profesortbaker

Thomas Jerome Baker

Connect with me on Facebook:
https://www.facebook.com/profesorbaker?ref=tn_tnmn

Connect with me on Linkedin:
http://www.linkedin.com/profile/view?id=12861148&trk=tab_pro

Check out my blog here: http://profesorbaker.com/

OTHER BOOKS BY THOMAS JEROME BAKER

http://www.amazon.com/Thomas-Jerome-Baker/e/B007G9HJFM

ONE LAST THING...

If you enjoyed this book, found it useful or helpful for you or a colleague in any way, I would be very grateful if you would write a short review on Amazon. Your support really does make a difference and I read all the reviews personally so I can get your feedback and make this book even better.

All you need to do is click the part where it says WRITE A REVIEW on this book's page on Amazon. I thank you most kindly for writing a kind review. Your support is valuable!

I'm wishing you the best of health, happiness and success! Here's to you!

Thomas Jerome Baker

Case Study: Maids of Misfortune

(Source: CreateSpaceBlogger)

M. Louisa Locke was on a 20-year quest to publish her Victorian mystery series. She finally found the avenue to get her books out into the world when she discovered independent publishing. By combining strategic marketing techniques with good storytelling and word-of-mouth, Louisa has gained fans and increased her book sales exponentially each year. Here, she shares the story of her publishing success and provides tips for her fellow indie authors.

Tell us about your book.

I have published 3 novels and 2 short stories in my ongoing series of mysteries set in Victorian San Francisco. I came up with the idea for the plot for the first book, Maids of Misfortune, more than 30 years ago while researching my doctoral dissertation on working women in western urban areas at the end of the 19th century. As I read a diary by a San Francisco live-in domestic servant of that period, I came up with the idea of a locked-door mystery. Ten years later, between my first teaching jobs, I decided to write the story. My protagonist, Annie Fuller, is a young widow who runs a boarding house and supplements that income as a fortune-teller. In Maids of Misfortune, she goes undercover as a domestic servant to investigate a crime. In the second book, Uneasy Spirits, she investigates fraudulent trance mediums, and in the most recent book, Bloody Lessons, Annie discovers who is sending poison pen letters about school teachers.

Care to share your author bio?

I knew from the age of 12 that I wanted to write historical fiction, but I assumed I would need a day job. When I graduated from college in the early 1970s, I decided to get a doctorate in history and become a college professor. I taught U.S. and U.S. women's history at San Diego Mesa College for more than 20 years. Although I thoroughly enjoyed my career, I continued to work on the draft of the historical mystery I had written years earlier.

In December 2009, after having semi-retired from teaching, I published that book in print with CreateSpace and as an eBook with Kindle Direct Publishing (KDP). Within a year, I was selling enough copies of *Maids of Misfortune* to retire completely from teaching and write and market full-time. I write frequently about my self-publishing journey and successful marketing strategies on my blog, and I am on the board of directors of the Historical Fiction Authors Cooperative. I live in San Diego with my husband while I work on the fourth book in my series.

How did you come to independent publishing?

When I wrote the first draft of *Maids of Misfortune* in 1989, I immediately got an agent. However, the consistent response by editors was that they weren't sure how strong the historical mystery market was. Of course, the market would prove very robust in the next decades. Then, in 2001 I entered into a three-year contract with a small press, but they didn't come through on their promises and never sold a single copy of my book.

I knew my book had potential, but I had become increasingly frustrated by my attempts to go the traditional route to publication.

I belonged to a writers group, and over the 20 years the group had been together, I had watched as friends who had been successful mid-list authors in the 1990s found their backlists out-of-print and their new books rejected by their editors and agents.

That's when I began to do research into indie publishing.

I attended a conference in 2009 where agents and publishers spoke about advances for new authors of genre books being less than $5000, that their policy was to delay releasing eBook editions for at least a year after the print editions were published, and that at the very minimum it would take 18 months for a book that was accepted to actually make it into print.

This contrasted with the exciting new possibilities about independent publishing being discussed online. The entrenched attitudes I encountered were so stark that I returned home and made my decision to self-publish *Maids of Misfortune*.

Life was too short and I was too old to wait for traditional publishing to catch up with the changes that I, for one, could see were coming to the industry. Best decision I ever made.

What brought you to CreateSpace and Kindle Direct Publishing (KDP)?

I was committed to doing everything myself (only spending money for a professionally designed cover), and the instructions for CreateSpace and KDP were straight-forward.

When KDP offered the 70% royalty split, my royalties increased dramatically, and I was delighted to get a steady monthly income. The development of the KDP Select program has probably been the most important tool for indie authors, as it can raise a book's visibility.

I think the best thing about Amazon's publishing platforms is that they are steadily improving. With my most recent book, I was particularly impressed by the book previewer. I also love that when I make changes to a book's price, keywords, product description, and so forth that the change happens quickly and the book continues to be available for sale.

Tell us about your marketing efforts. How did you get the word out about your book?

I used Twitter, my Facebook author page, and my blog to announce the availability of my latest book, Bloody Lessons. I put the print copy of the book up as a giveaway on Goodreads. I sent out an email to all the fans who contacted me over the past three years and told them the book was now available and asked them to sign up for my newsletter. I also contacted professional review bloggers who had reviewed my previous books and offered to send them copies. I ended up with solid, professional reviews and have gotten many more positive customer reviews on Amazon.com, which I know will continue to help sell the book.

On the day of the launch, I made the first book in the series, Maids of Misfortune, free for three days via KDP Select and discounted the sequel, *Uneasy Spirits*, to 99 cents for a week. By combining these promotions, I was able to point out that a reader could get all three eBooks in the series for under $5, knowing that this would attract readers who had not yet heard of the series. In the first two weeks of publication, I held a contest on my Facebook author page where I gave away $5 Amazon gift certificates to the first people who could answer trivia questions about the new book. I also participated in a virtual book tour that took me to seven book blogger sites. As a result of all these marketing strategies, *Bloody Lessons* has continuously shown up on the bestseller lists in multiple categories.

What are your goals with your book project?

When I first published *Maids of Misfortune*, my goal was to give a book that I had worked on for 20 years a chance to be read. Once this book achieved success, I became motivated by fans who wanted to know what was going to happen next to my protagonist.

However, my underlying goal has always been to figure out a way to make the information I had learned about 19th-century working women available in an entertaining and accessible fashion. I firmly believe that without the opportunity to self-publish that CreateSpace and KDP have given me, none of that would be possible.

What have been some of your biggest successes so far?

I have been independently published for nearly four years, and every year I have been more successful than the last. For the past two years, my income has been greater than my income as a full professor at the peak of my teaching career.

What advice would you offer your fellow authors?

I think the key to being an indie author (besides making sure your book meets professional standards in editing, cover design, and product description) is to keep up with the changing marketing landscape and be willing to experiment.

Authors should subscribe to the numerous blogs or forums that talk about marketing to hear about new promotional tools early. Also, authors need to be persistent, since sometimes they experiment with something once, and if the results don't live up to their expectations, they will never try again. Many authors also don't bother to experiment with categories, fill out their Author Central profiles, or invest in a promotion campaign. If no one hears about a book through word-of-mouth (and social media) or it doesn't show up near the top in any browsing category, it doesn't matter how good the book is - no one is going to buy it. Authors must be willing to self-promote if they want their books read.

19395951R00058

Printed in Poland
by Amazon Fulfillment
Poland Sp. z o.o., Wrocław